THE ROOM

THE ROOM
THE DEFINITIVE GUIDE

RYAN FINNIGAN

APPLAUSE
THEATRE & CINEMA BOOKS

An Imprint of Hal Leonard Corporation

Published in 2014 by Applause Theatre & Cinema Books
An Imprint of Hal Leonard Corporation
7777 West Bluemound Road
Milwaukee, WI 53213

Trade Book Division Editorial Offices
33 Plymouth St., Montclair, NJ 07042

Printed in the United States of America

Book design by Mute

Library of Congress Cataloging-in-Publication Date is available upon request.

ISBN 978-1-4803-9096-6

www.applausebooks.com

CONTENTS

Preface   vii
Acknowledgments   xi
Introduction: The *Room* Phenomenon   xiii

Part One: "Apprehension"—A Viewer's Guide
1 How to Handle Entering *The Room*   3
2 How to Throw a Spoon: The Viewer's Guide   5
3 How to Discover a Cult Phenomenon   15
    MICHAEL ROUSSELET
4 How to Infect Others with the *Room* Virus   21
    JAMES DURKIN
5 How to Talk to Your Friends About Becoming a Fan of *The Room*   25
    STEVE HEISLER
6 How to Watch *The Room* if You're Juliette Danielle   29
    JULIETTE DANIELLE

Part Two: "Comprehension"—Analysis and Interviews
7 10x10: Dissecting *The Room,* Part One: 0:00:00–0:09:04   37
    ALAN JONES
8 Lisa: Juliette Danielle Interview   43
9 10x10, Part Two: 0:09:05–0:20:33   47
    ALAN JONES
10 Denny: Philip Haldiman Interview   55
11 10x10, Part Three: 0:20:34–0:29:23   59
    ALAN JONES
12 The Flower Shop Scene   65
13 10x10, Part Four: 0:29:24–0:40:01   67
    ALAN JONES
14 Chris-R: Dan Janjigian Interview   75
15 10x10, Part Five: 0:40:02–0:49:09   79
    ALAN JONES
16 Michelle: Robyn Paris Interview   85
17 10x10, Part Six: 0:49:10–1:00:57   91
    ALAN JONES
18 Peter: Kyle Vogt Interview   99

19 10x10, Part Seven: 1:00:58–1:10:00   **103**
    ALAN JONES

20 The Music of *The Room:* Mladen Milicevic and Clint Jun Gamboa
    Interviews   **109**

21 10x10, Part Eight: 1:10:01–1:19:53   **115**
    ALAN JONES

22 Steven: Greg Ellery Interview   **121**

23 10x10, Part Nine: 1:19:54–1:30:36   **125**
    ALAN JONES

24 Citizen Johnny: Welles vs. Wiseau   **131**

25 10x10, Part Ten: 1:30:37–1:39:35   **133**
    ALAN JONES

Part Three: "Obsession"—Life outside *The Room*

26 The Further Works of Tommy Wiseau   **141**

27 Greg Sestero, *The Disaster Artist* and Beyond   **159**

28 The Best of the Extended *Room*niverse   **167**

Epilogue: The Future of *The Room*   **181**

Notes   **183**

Sources   **189**

PREFACE

Five years ago, I was completely oblivious to *The Room*. Just after the film had its UK premiere in London, I traveled to Leeds to view a copy of it owned by my good friend James Durkin. The viewing was astonishing—a total epiphany—and the prototype for many, many others that would follow: we drank, laughed, cowered, screamed, cringed, winced, laughed some more, and cried out "what the . . . ?!" multiple times. Mostly, though, we laughed, and then, before we knew it, it was all over—although, naturally, we then went on to talk about it for the rest of the night.

I had so many questions. Had he seen all of that weird stuff, too? That couldn't have been for real . . . right? What had we just been through together? Who *are* these people—and, especially, who the hell is this Tommy Wiseau guy—anyway? Everything we had learned together as students of film was now completely out of the window, and in one hundred minutes, almost every single rule of narrative filmmaking as we knew it had been broken. This was something unique.

Traveling home with this sensational viewing fresh in my mind, I was ready to tell everyone about *The Room*. I showed the film to the people I lived with, and they fell in love with it. We showed it to our extended group of friends, and they all fell in love, too. I didn't throw a spoon until three years later, when a screening was finally scheduled in Sheffield, at a small, eighty-seat theater. I immediately booked ten tickets, without having yet asked anyone to come with me. Then I booked some more, just in case. I was going to drag along anyone I could to see the film on the big screen.

We had gotten somewhat drunk on the way, and there was already an electric mood of excitement between us even before we'd entered the foyer that night. When we arrived at the theater, there were a lot of familiar faces around, people we recognized but couldn't quite place, as well as a few others we hadn't seen for years. It felt like a *moment* of some kind.

That night, *The Room* became an entirely new film for us all. In the intervening years, we had read about some of the customs of screenings, but we weren't about to act them out in our living rooms. Here, though, as soon as the movie started, there was practically a riot. As someone who had been brought up to believe that the cinema was a solemn place of worship—to be respectful of it at all times, and, most of all, to never make a sound during a film—I had never seen anything like it. As hyperbolic as it may sound, this was my Sex Pistols at the Manchester Lesser Free Trade Hall.

I later met the organizer of the screening, Matt Risby, and before long we had started our own cult-film night, offering event screenings around the city. We named it the Five and Dime Picture Show, and when it came to programming our first season of films, a repeat screening of *The Room* was the very first thing we decided upon. It was a decision made in seconds.

Over a period of four months, we devised a plan to top the first screening, in a bigger venue. We dealt directly and extensively with Wiseau-Films, and Tommy himself kindly provided us with signed merchandise to give away. Greg Sestero recorded a video introduction to the film; our designer, Mute, created a poster and a "Viewer's Guide" for the audience; we wrote a pre-screening presentation about the film; stickers were made for *Room* virgins; and spoons, footballs, fancy dress, and games were all in abundance. To build excitement for the screening, Alan Jones and I wrote a series of articles about the film and its tenth anniversary for my website, [SIC] Blog, including interviews with cast members Juliette Danielle and Philip Haldiman. Overall, it was a major operation, and when we finally opened the doors it was almost exactly one year to the day since Matt's previous screening. This time, not 80 but 280 people turned up, and it was by far our most successful screening that year—and one of the best nights of my life.

I'm opening this book by talking about my own experiences because, in many ways, *The Room* has infected my life. I hope what I have just shown is that *The Room* has formed the basis of new friendships, and also strengthened existing ones. All of the friends I have singled out and named above worked on this book, bringing us even closer together, while many new friendships have formed along the way.

It goes without saying that a few people who know me have offered genuine concern for my wellbeing during the period in which the film has seemed to increasingly occupy my time (culminating in this book). This is mainly because, to an outsider, becoming a huge fan of a film—or anything else—that is considered among the very worst in its field can be a confusing concept. In writing this book, I have spoken to and interviewed fellow "Roomies," "Roomantics," and "Wi-Hards," and I now know for certain what I had always suspected: that these are typical experiences for people who fall for the film. In fact, by comparison to some, they are extremely tame examples of *Room* fandom. Some people look forward to Christmas all year round; others follow Bob Dylan around the country on tour, or take annual vacations to the same place each year. For us, it's all about going to see Tommy Wiseau's masterpiece on a regular basis.

As someone who has never written a book before, I believe now that I have subconsciously been inspired by—and worked in—the Wiseau-way. Like *The Room,* this is the project of a first-timer, fueled by a passion to deliver an end product under the guidance of a company that knows its industry well and has—figuratively, at least—allowed me to shoot in its parking lot. Like Tommy, I have recognized my own limitations and invited contributors and collaborators to help in areas where my own knowledge and skills are lacking, and have naively fumbled my way through making each element of these things happen. (I guess the big difference is that I didn't have $6 million to make it happen, but then you can't have everything.)

My aim for this book is to capture some of the spirit of the film and the experience. I hope that this book introduces the film to new fans, but also that it is of interest to other fanatics. More than anything, I hope that it is even a tiny bit as much fun as *The Room.*

Ryan Finnigan
April 2014

* * *

Ryan Finnigan is a freelance writer who has written for a number of publications on the subject of film while also working as the editor of [SIC] Blog, a website focused on alternative, independent, and cult films. Outside of writing, Ryan forms one half of the Five and Dime Picture Show, programming and hosting event screenings of cult films in Sheffield. He graduated from Sheffield Hallam University with a degree in film studies in 2006, and currently works for the university's internal communications network.

Firstly, I would like to thank John Cerullo and the team at Hal Leonard for understanding what makes *The Room* special, and for having the initial faith in Mute and me, as well as offering invaluable support and guidance along the way. As ever, endless gratitude and thanks goes to my family and friends for their support, and especially Rebecca Mason.

This book has been made possible by the generous contributions and time given by a great number of people. I deeply thank Mute for bringing his vision, optimism, and talent to whatever we work on together, and for embarking upon this journey with me.

Extra special thanks goes to Alan Jones, James Durkin, Michael Rousselet, Steve Heisler, and Juliette Danielle, for embracing and supporting the project and contributing their unique wit, humor, and intelligence to the book, thus raising it beyond my own limits. Additionally, I would like to thank Thomas John, Tom Morton, Kathryn Webb, and Jacob Millen-Bamford, for their valuable behind the scenes support.

Heartfelt and warm thanks go to the incredible people I have had the pleasure to interview from *The Room,* and the community surrounding the film. Their knowledge, wisdom, and support has informed and propelled this book, and I extend a special thank you to all of them, including: Greg Sestero, Juliette Danielle, Philip Haldiman, Kyle Vogt, Dan Janjigian, Robyn Paris, Greg Ellery, Mladen Milicevic, Clint Jun Gamboa, Paul Scheer, Payman Benz, Brock LaBorde, Ian Berry, Will Moglia, Branden Kong, Jennifer Lieberman, Elias Eliot, Rick Harper, Matt Downey, Tom Fulp, Greg DeLiso, Mark Breese, Peter Litvin, Alison Goertz, Timon Singh, Matt Risby, and Danielle Bacher.

Lastly, and most importantly, I would like to thank Tommy Wiseau. Without *The Room,* none of this would have been possible; countless great times and friendships wouldn't have existed; and the world would certainly be a much worse place to live. Thank you.

INTRODUCTION: THE *ROOM* PHENOMENON

"The distance between insanity and genius is measured only by success."—BRUCE FEIRSTEIN[1]

In 2003, an independently produced film made with a $6 million budget was released into the world under the unassuming title of *The Room.* The film was written, produced, and directed by an unknown and unconventional man by the name of Tommy Wiseau, who cast himself as its central character, Johnny. The initial release of *The Room* was met with mixed reviews. The small amount of them that were positive read disingenuously, while the overwhelmingly negative ones panned it. One review from the day after the film's premiere in June of that year described it as a "big, steaming nut-filled turd," likening the act of watching it to "getting stabbed in the head."[2]

Strangely, the film would eventually find an audience to embrace it and all of its faults, and despite its reputation as one of the worst films ever made, *The Room* can now be seen as one of the most successful films of the twenty-first century so far. Having evolved into a global success, it has been theatrically exhibited continually since its release, finding rabid audiences worldwide, and has passed into the realms of bona-fide pop-culture phenomenon, its devoted fan base growing with each passing year. A level of audience participation has developed that's comparable only with that of the original midnight-movie cult film, *The Rocky Horror Picture Show,* and the desire to see the film in a communal environment has resulted in a vast multitude of large-scale sell-out screenings, each filled with tears of laughter and a sense of joy that is hard to find elsewhere.

So what exactly is *The Room* about? Well, that's actually kind of a tough question. Part of what makes the film so brilliantly unique is that it is almost completely inept by all standards of conventional filmmaking and narrative storytelling. A brief attempt at a synopsis would be that Johnny, a successful banker, is living the American dream with his beautiful wife-to-be, Lisa, and their adopted . . . neighbor/surrogate son/friend (?!), the inimitable Denny. However, Johnny's world is turned upside down when Lisa has an affair with his best friend, Mark. Denny briefly gets involved with drugs. Lisa's mother gets breast cancer . . . and it is never mentioned again. Many characters come in and out of the film, some of whom are never actually introduced. There are entire scenes that don't make sense, and . . . let's just say that a whole other bunch of seemingly random, nonsensical things happen before the film reaches its conclusion, with Johnny discovering Lisa's affair.

It would be an understatement to say that the film is incompetent. However, part of the charm of *The Room* is in witnessing Wiseau's sincere attempt at making a profound and meaningful movie—an attempt that falls so far wide of the mark that it barely seems possible. The dialogue, scenarios, and performances are of an unprecedented level of ineptitude, with plotlines, characters, and even beards disappearing throughout. Continuity is dire, scenes are repeated, the soundtrack doesn't fit and . . . well, we could be here all day. However, what is clear is that Wiseau's film is an autobiographical tale of betrayal and despair, and a clear attempt to impart wisdom—and that it may also have been intended to settle a couple of personal scores.

In one of the film's most sincere attempts at poignancy, Johnny states, "If a lot of people love each other, the world would be a better place to live," and within the parameters of the film, this is as completely surreal and out of place as anything else. However, in reality, these words could easily sum up the joy, companionship, and sense of communal experience that the film brings, as well as the communities that have grown around it. To some, *The Room* might only be the worst film ever made, which means it is of little-to-no significance to them. To others, it's a shared experience, a night out, and/or one of the funniest things of all time—something that brings a huge amount of happiness. Of course, there's also a further group who think the film is actually an excellent piece of work by a calculating genius ahead of his time—and, who knows, they may even be right.

The success of *The Room* can be seen as fitting into a larger, developing lust for bad filmmaking, and the growing popularity of comedic viewings of such titles throughout cinema history, with *Reefer Madness, Plan 9 from Outer Space, Manos: The Hands of Fate, Howard the Duck, Showgirls,* and *Gigli* being just some of hundreds of ironically popular titles. For some, it seems that the celebration and understanding of what makes great cinema is complemented by a recognition of the projects that fall short in meeting these standards. The films celebrated and watched in this fashion are not merely average but are actually extremely poor or misguided attempts at greatness, although in entertaining their audience, they can be effectively enjoyed as unintentional comedy—or, to quote the oft-used phrase, "So bad it's good."

This is certainly not a new craze, however, with the comedic value of bad movies having been popularized back in 1978, in the book *The*

Fifty Worst Films of All Time (And How They Got That Way),[3] and made more prominent with the emergence of the Golden Raspberry Awards, or "Razzies," which have celebrated the worst of Hollywood since 1980. However, the dawn of the Internet has allowed for the viral sharing of clips from hilariously bad films, allowing new viewers to taste the films for free, and online fan culture has turned formerly marginalized movies into accessible entities.

In the early '90s, shows like *Mystery Science Theater 3000* pioneered comedic "riffing" on the shortcomings of such films, and by the turn of the twenty-first century, savage reviews of subpar films, such as the Red Letter Media dissection of *Star Wars Episode I: The Phantom Menace,* were becoming Internet sensations.[4] At this point in time, bad filmmaking has become a part of the cultural zeitgeist, with the comedy show *Garth Marenghi's Darkplace* intentionally spoofing the grammar of cinematic mistakes, and films like *Snakes on a Plane, Machete,* and *Sharknado* knowingly adopting B-movie qualities. Furthermore, original "classics" of the genre, such as *Troll 2,* are now celebrated, and the intrigue surrounding their production and backstories have become the subject of fascination and celebration in themselves. (The star of *Troll 2,* Michael Stephenson, made a popular documentary about the creation of the film, *Best Worst Movie,* in 2009.)

The Room has generated much the same level of interest, and the further you delve into it, the more everything returns to one thing: Tommy Wiseau. Everything that is truly unique about the film—good or bad— originated solely from him, and many viewers have gone to great lengths to discover more about the man. As a person, he undoubtedly has an almost magical, mythical appeal, and there remains a compelling mystery surrounding him and the circumstances that led to the production and completion of *The Room.* That's not surprising, given that this tale of a self-financed production with a large amount of money from unknown sources, secured by a director whose nationality, age, and background are unclear, has the making of a great mystery-thriller novel. Over the years, various details have slipped out and only further confused those trying to make sense of the film and its existence: odd details, including that the film was shot on both 35 mm film and HD formats concurrently,[5] and of further idiosyncratic practices, such as the casting of understudies for each role, as if anticipating the possibility of actors leaving the set or being fired from the film—which they did, and were. Information such as this begins to explain the condition of the final film by scratching the surface of the circumstantial ingredients involved in the catastrophic chaos of Wiseau's production, yet it also just raised further questions, all of which could be distilled into one recurring, overarching question: why?

Once the film had found an initial audience willing to make a mockery out of a melodrama, Wiseau remarketed *The Room* as a "black comedy."

Although this was significant for him in embracing the new appeal of the film, it's unlikely that the rebranding meant anything to anyone else (other than further lengthening the list of Wiseau idiosyncrasies, that is). The most effective marketing of the film remains the word-of-mouth passing of it on to others by audiences and programmers. A savvy and determined businessman, Wiseau chose to redefine his film and meet audiences in the middle, following the logic that all laughter is good laughter:

> **If you have a good comedy . . . how they say "good" comedy, again how you define "good" is a question mark, because I can define this way, somebody else can define something differently, but on the end of the day, we come out to the same conclusion, because why? Because we be laughing.[6]**

As an artist, Wiseau is admirably malleable, and happy for audiences to interpret his work as they wish, while remaining defiantly assured in his belief that everything in *The Room* "was intentional" and planned from the beginning.[7] His ability to talk around a problem—or talk someone who disagrees with him into complete confusion—is one of his great gifts as a salesman. That he still seems genuinely enamored with the finished product and able to defend the story, production, and intentions behind *The Room* is testament to his grand delusion. If we are to take Wiseau on his word that *The Room* is exactly the film he intended it to be, though, then the appeal of the finished product becomes extremely complex, and it really could be the work of a true genius.

This book, then, is your entry into what can be a puzzling world of fanaticism. It is an attempt to explore the phenomenon of *The Room* by looking at the things that make it unique, while also attempting to retain the sense of humor that makes the film so infectious. If you've never entered *The Room* before, then you need to get hold of the film, right now, watch it, and then take yourself to a screening as soon as possible.[8]

Part one of the book looks at the act of viewing, interacting with, and sharing the film with others, and explains certain viewing customs for newcomers. Providing unique perspective and insight on the film in this section are a number of guest contributors, including principle cast member Juliette Danielle; the originator of the spoon-throwing ritual, Michael Rousselet; and a key expert on the film, Steve Heisler.

Part two offers a satirical look at the details of the film itself, in ten minute sections, by Alan Jones, in his *10x10: Dissecting The Room.* By focusing on the key scenes and their motivations, these chapters not only provide a brutally funny overview but also look deeper into the appeal of *The Room* and show how a film that shouldn't work actually does work for so many. These chapters are separated by interviews with key members of the cast and crew about their experiences of working on the film and the cult following it has gained.

Finally, part three looks at how the life of *The Room* has extended beyond the film itself, attempts to understand Tommy Wiseau with an analysis of his further work, and also looks at the international bestseller that *The Room* inspired, *The Disaster Artist,* by cast member Greg Sestero and co-author Tom Bissell. There are extensive interviews in this section with notable fans, artists, and collaborators on Tommy Wiseau's other projects, including *The Tommy Wi-Show* and his mysterious sitcom, *The Neighbors.*

In unraveling *The Room* as a film and a social phenomenon while also looking at its creators and fans, what lies within these pages should hopefully allow some further understanding of how a film that should never have been remembered has become something of longevity and influence. For the purpose of transparency, though, it is worth stating now that a full understanding of *The Room* may be something that is never achieved by anybody. Ever.

THE ROOM

PART ONE

"APPREHENSION"

A VIEWER'S GUIDE

We're all born *Room* virgins, and that's a fact!

It's something that you shouldn't be ashamed of, but it can be a difficult period of transition for anyone. You may experience certain "stages" when you first experience *The Room*. These vary from person to person, and you might not go through all of them, but here's a handy guide to help you through.

Stage One: Shock
You have never seen anything like this before, and you don't know how to react. Relax! It's just a film, and everyone else is just as scared as you are, first time out. You will experience heavy confusion, feelings of memory loss and/or lapses in logic, and occasional feelings of nausea for approximately one hundred minutes. Keep calm. It will pass.

Stage Two: Awe
Having now entered *The Room,* you will find what you have just experienced has made a lasting impression on you. It may have seemed like a bad experience at the time, but now you find yourself wanting to do it again. This is perfectly normal, and it's predicted that some viewers will repeat the experience regularly for the rest of their lives. (As yet, no long-term studies exist.)

Stage Three: Wonder

What you are now experiencing is the euphoric feeling that results from throwing off conventions and logic. You feel liberated, having accepted the film for what it is and moved beyond mockery and revulsion into a celebration and conscious deeper exploration, admiring every small detail.

Stage Four: Empathy

Fascination and sheer glee have compelled you to philosophically explore what lies beneath the foundations of *The Room,* the motivations behind it, and the history of its conception. You may experience minor feelings of guilt, for ever questioning or deriding anybody within the film, and a side effect may be to overcompensate for this by exclaiming *The Room's* greatness to others, or through buying an extensive range of merchandise.

Stage Five: Understanding

In extreme cases, you may now think that *The Room* is actually the best film of all time and profess a deep connection to it. At this point, others may question your sanity. As a stage five inhabitant, it is important to remember that these people are at a lower stage of being than you. Help them by encouraging them to revisit the film, or by repeating the wise(au) words of its creator, and eventually they will come around—or leave you alone.

2

HOW TO
THROW A SPOON

THE VIEWER'S GUIDE

"The Room is not a movie—IT IS THE EVENT!"—Tommy Wiseau[1]

In choosing to view *The Room* in a theater, you will be entering into a world of customs that have been evolving since 2003, when the seeds of cult fandom were planted by a group of friends in Los Angeles, led by Michael Rousselet. To briefly explain to a newcomer: theatrical screenings of *The Room* have a number of "rituals," through which the audience can interact with the film. Before discussing these, however, it is important to note that they have evolved over time, and part of what makes viewing the film such fun is that, rather than there being a rigid set of laws that you have to observe, each screening is different, with certain regions and individuals bringing their own jokes, props, ideas, quips, and surrounding events to the screenings.

The number-one Tommy Wiseau catchphrase—and his overriding philosophy regarding *The Room* screenings—must surely be, "You can laugh, you can cry, you can express yourself, but please, don't hurt each other!"[2] It's a great mantra to observe. It is important to note, in the interest of objectivity, that the quality of each screening is dependent on the quality of its audience. From the number of screenings I have attended, and from the research I have undertaken, it would seem as though there are a number of unwritten rules to keep proceedings from descending into chaos. An audience is encouraged to shout out jokes, although it's generally accepted that you leave your stupid comments in your pocket during the film's key scenes, and accept some general shushing. No matter how good a comedian you are, you're not as funny as Tommy Wiseau, and you never will be.

If you're viewing the film for the first time in a theater, it's possible to feel a little bit lost, and because of the general raucousness of the screening, you may miss a lot of what's happening, first time round. Audience members often seek out the film to watch alone before attending their first screening. Ian Berry of Cinema 21 in Portland, Oregon, even actively encourages audiences to watch the film alone first:

> I always recommend watching the film at home before coming to a public screening. This is such an odd thing to say about such a bad movie, but there are so many wonderful details and nuances in the piece that are very easy to overlook when caught up in the pageantry of the public screenings.[3]

Don't fret if you can't see the film at home first, though. A good host will often introduce the film and point out how you can get involved. Also, one of the remarkably fortuitous elements of *The Room* is that the repetitive structure of it will allow you to pick up the film's customs just by observing those around you. Dan Janjigian, who plays Chris-R in *The Room,* says of the screenings, "If you've never seen [*The Room*], kind of just let yourself go with it. If people are doing stuff around you, let yourself get drawn into it. This is a day when you want to give in to peer pressure."[4]

If you are one of the fastidious *Room* virgins who wants to bone up on the screening rituals before you go ahead and see the movie, though, what follows is a short guide to just some of the things you can expect to experience, as well as a few pointers of things to keep an eye out for. See, *The Room* is like a modern-day folk song, with viewers taking elements of the things they see at screenings and making them their own.

Elias Eliot, one of Europe's most notable *Room* programmers and screening hosts, offers up the following advice:

> There are so many rituals surrounding this movie, but don't tell people what to do. Let them find out by themselves. It needs to be natural. I think that is always part of why it's successful, because it's an organic thing; people need to realize these things themselves. We did hang a rule book, or whatever you'd call it, on the wall for people to read by themselves, but I never told people what to do.[5]

Things You'll Need to Know About

Proceed through these sections as you wish, but as our hero Johnny says, "Don't plan too much." If *The Room* is to teach you anything, it's that there's no point in thinking ahead about what movie you're going to see.

Spoons

The throwing of plastic spoons has become customary at screenings of *The Room,* and is the most famous of the rituals associated with the film. Upon noticing that Johnny's apartment is ineptly decorated with a number of items, including cheap, framed stock photos of spoons (which Wiseau bought in real life from a thrift store[6]), audiences began to follow Michael Rousselet's lead and shout out "Spoooooon!" while throwing their spoons toward the screen—or at each other—whenever they appear onscreen.

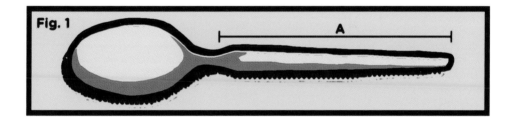

The theoretical absurdity of the characters in the film leaving stock images of spoons in their frames, rather than replacing them with photos of their own—and the audience's hanging on to this as a singular point representing the skewed layer of superficiality and unnatural behavior of the people within the film—hints at the deeper level of meaning behind the spoon throwing. However, Tommy Wiseau offers his own explanation of the use of plastic spoons—which he says are symbolic of how "plastic is harmful to your body," adding that the development of non-toxic alternatives represents "survival as well, think about it . . . what we can do to improve."[7] I must admit that, while I have thought about this a great deal, I'm still not sure I quite get it.

Top Tip: Make sure you take a number of spoons with you, as there are plenty of opportunities to throw them around. Also, if you're sitting near the front of the theater, be a good Roomie and throw some back from the pool at the front.

The Sex Scenes

Aside from the spoons, one of the truly very most important things that avid fans feel most compelled to point out to the newcomer is the gratuitous nature of the sex scenes in the film. There are three sex scenes within the first twenty-six minutes, and as comedian Paul Scheer points out, "One of the sex scenes occurs eight minutes in, and is four minutes long,"[8] which means that it makes up one-third of the film at that point. If you can make it past these scenes, the film becomes a much more pleasurable experience.

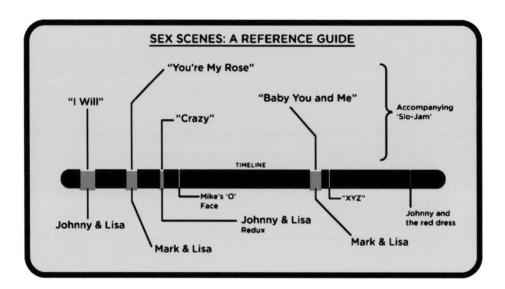

Footballs

Football—and/or "tossing the ball around"—pops up throughout *The Room* for seemingly no real reason, often within extremely confined spaces and at inappropriate times, resulting in preposterous injuries for the characters of Mike and Peter. The bizarre recurrence of footballs in the film means they have become a key *Room* meme, while the ball itself can be seen as a key example of Wiseau's love of his adopted American culture. The misappropriation of it gives it another level of meaning: that of an outsider's misunderstanding of a tradition, and/or the need to adopt something into a form more open to their involvement.

For Wiseau, the symbolism of the football seems to relate largely to the concept of freedom of choice in America, and the experimentation that liberty allows. He has explained his thought process as, "'Wait a minute? Can they play football in tuxedo? Hmm . . . why not? Let's try it!' That's what we did!"[9] Obviously, it's pretty dangerous—and silly—to throw real footballs around at screenings in the manner of the spoons, as demonstrated by the YouTube video "Tommy Wiseau gets hit by Football."[10] Savvy audiences will take along a soft, foam football and head to the front of the theater to toss it around at the same time as the characters onscreen, or just instigate some ball throwing afterward.

Top Tip: If you're attending a screening with Wiseau in attendance, stick around outside afterward for a game of football with the man himself.

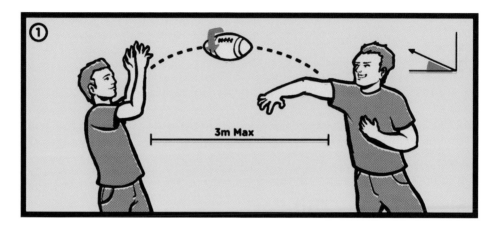

Tuxedos and Costumes

Many things appear and disappear in *The Room* without much logical explanation, and the largely unexplained wearing of tuxedos by the central male characters as they play football in the "wedding photos" scene has become a key example of the perceived "randomness" of the film. An experienced Roomie might point out that Peter's injury in the tuxedo-football scene is a foreshadowing of Johnny and Lisa's doomed relationship, and the inability of their marriage to "go long." But that person may be crazy.

Most importantly, the tuxedo presents *The Room* audience with one of many opportunities to join in by dressing in costume. Aside from the tuxedo, the film offers a number of peculiar fashions for fans to adopt at screenings, including Lisa's "sexy" red dress, Mark's double denim, and Chris-R's beanie/goatee combo.

Top Tip: Try to find something creative to dress as. Sure, it's cool to dress up as Johnny, but why not go one further and dress as a gigantic spoon or a piece of cheesecake?

Ways to Join In

If you're looking for some shortcuts to understanding some of the things you may hear or want to join in with while watching *The Room,* here are some of the key points.

- Saying "Oh hai!" any time Johnny does, and/or when a character enters. See also: "Shut the door!"
- Laughing along with Tommy Wiseau's deranged laugh: "HA HA HA!"
- Counting things like the number of homoerotic football passes Johnny and Mark make in their Top Gun-esque scene, and/or the number of times Mark says "best friend."
- Calling "Focus!" if the film goes out of focus. (Hint: it does.)
- "Grossing out" during the sex scenes.
- Chanting "Go! Go! Go!" during the Golden Gate Bridge cutaways.

Top Tip: If you want to attend a screening and progress straight to Expert Mode, find out when and why to shout "One . . . Two . . . FUCK IT!" and when to get Johnny to wave to you at the bottom right-hand corner of the screen.

Things to Look Out For

The Room is, surprisingly, a densely layered work, and for many it takes several viewings for the full wonders littered throughout to become apparent. Here, you will find a list of things to look out for. See if you can spot them all.

> San Francisco . . . literally all of it.
> Johnny on tram
> An extra present appearing on the sofa
> World's first bellybutton sex
> Repeat sex scene (aka "Pee break")
> The impossible rooftop
> Money (where is it?)
> Drugs (but what kind?)
> "ARGGGH, WHAT IS WRONG WITH LISA'S NECK!?"
> "ME UNDERWEARS!"
> Worst accidents ever (more than one)
> Weird blue donkey
> SCOTCHKA. Yum.
> #everydaysexism

What to Expect at a Screening of *The Room*

The film itself—and the audience participation it inspires—forms the major component of what makes the theatrical experience so enjoyable. But the fun doesn't have to stop there, and you may want to strap in for some extra content. Programmers will often throw in an introduction to the film, and to Wiseau himself. They might choose to show extra video content, like music videos (see "The Best of the Extended *Room*niverse" for examples), or hold competitions, giveaways, and contests to add to the festive atmosphere. Undoubtedly, the biggest draw at screenings of *The Room* is the fact that they are often accompanied by personal appearances by Wiseau, sometimes with Greg Sestero and other members of the cast in tow. Given that Wiseau independently distributed the film, it's no surprise that he has continued to keep a close eye on its performance, and is aware of how his presence can bring larger audiences to screenings.

People flock to see Wiseau because he is a natural entertainer, and over the years he has developed a well-oiled approach to screenings. He will arrive at the theater to greet the lines of waiting fans, hold court pre-screening to sell official merchandise, sign memorabilia, and then conduct a question-and-answer session in the theater. It's been noted that Wiseau is evasive when answering audience questions, which are often met with the words, "Move on, next question," and he can be impatient with those not forthcoming with their questions. On one occasion, in response to a question posed by the Bristol Bad Film Club, he said, "No statement given, just Plain English 101. Question, which is— "how are you?" . . . Question mark. We don't want a statement."[11] Luckier fans may find him in a more jovial, co-operative mood, and may enjoy freebies, the aforementioned football throwing, and maybe even one of his memorable recitations of a Shakespeare sonnet.[12]

The atmosphere at screenings of *The Room*—and the roulette-like nature of the improvised fun that the film promises—has led to people returning to see it repeatedly, with the film often forming part of an evening out. For some cinemagoers, part of the appeal is the opportunity to invent their own customs upon viewing the film repeatedly, and a keenness to try out their best lines, props, and costumes on their unsuspecting peers, making *The Room* the figurehead of an exciting new interactive cinema experience.

How to Screen *The Room*

Once you have been to see *The Room* in the theater, you may find yourself inspired to host your own screening, which will begin with you contacting the good folk at Wiseau-Films. Upon making initial contact, you will find your e-mails answered by a man by the name of "John, Adm."[13] For some, this has proven to be a frustrating experience. As Timon Singh of the Bristol Bad Film Club explains, "I was emailing him every other week for a response, and if I did get one back, it was asking for the same details I had already provided. In the end, we reached out to clubs who had previously screened *The Room* and asked for their advice. Their solution—tell him you have the money ready to go!"[14]

In attempting to gain the rights to show the film and pay for the license, be prepared for some interesting questions. Here, Matt Risby of the Five and Dime Picture Show relates his experience with Wiseau-Films:

> Getting the license to screen *The Room* is a rigmarole and no mistake. The first time I screened it was for a small audience in a theater in England that holds eighty people. Having explained this and described the venue and its facilities in detail, John/Tommy countered, asking me to consider a bigger venue, perhaps something above 1,000 seats, perhaps in Berlin. He then followed up with possible promotional flyers I could make and where I should distribute them—around Germany.[15]

Once you have secured permission to screen *The Room,* it is your job to promote your screening. Marketing materials will be sent to you by Wiseau-Films, and will, of course, be quite unique. In fact, they will likely largely comprise of a number of Tommy Wiseau self portraits and headshots of varying quality, with some giving the impression that he has just stepped out of the shower before pouting into his camera-phone. In the event that you should want to create your own poster, it is advisable to run your original artwork past Wiseau-Films. When I screened the film myself, I commissioned the designer of this book, Mute, to create an original poster. Upon running this image by Wiseau-Films, I immediately received an e-mail from "John, Adm." with the subject "You Poster!??":

> Please note that your the poster is very brutal with TW's face; enclosed you will find sample of better picture. We understand that you try to make a point however it is not smooth. (you make TW's 200 year old??). Our suggestion will be if you can change that will be better.[16]

One of the pictures attached to the e-mail was a cartoon; another was a copy of the Blu-ray cover art. When I later met Wiseau, he "lovingly" strangled me in retaliation for the poster, for an uncomfortably long time. Let that be a warning to you.

Of course, you will also have the decision to make as to how to screen the film. Initially, the delayed home release of *The Room* might have been seen as a contributing factor to the popularity of theatrical screenings, although audiences at screenings have continued to grow since its release on DVD in 2005, and on Blu-ray in 2012. In fact, it seems that these releases have actually contributed to making the film easier to show, particularly in areas where 35 mm prints are hard to come by, or are not an option. The remastered Blu-ray transfer will also ensure that the film enjoys a life span beyond the original prints.

Not content with simply releasing the film, Wiseau has always included extra content for fans, and in fact the DVD and Blu-ray have different special features—another clever marketing technique to re-sell the film to the fanatics, perhaps, or maybe the chance to right initial wrongs, such as the infamously dubbed "Interview with Tommy Wiseau" from the DVD, in which a number of his responses are confusingly replaced by new answers that were recorded later. Perhaps the most interesting feature to be included on the Blu-ray is the "World's first combo languages" option, which gives the viewer the ability to display two different sets of subtitles at the same time. It's not quite clear what Wiseau intended with this, or whether it will ever be required, but it's the sort of eccentric forward thinking that has typified his approach to making *The Room* appeal to a global audience.

Having finally succeeded in getting your screening together, and an audience through the doors, it's your time to shine and put your own spin on *The Room* experience. The final piece of advice comes from Elias Eliot:

> **Do something different every time—we throw pillows to the audience so they have pillow fights during the movie. When I was in the States with the [*Disaster Artist*] launch I went to a screening in San Francisco, and they took balloons there. They could take our pillow idea and I could take their balloon idea.**[17]

Remember all the things you have learned from other screenings, get advice from other people in the *Room* community, and be prepared to be forever responsible for introducing somebody to *The Room* for the first time—and contemplate whether you will ever be able to sleep comfortably in that knowledge.

3

HOW TO
DISCOVER A CULT PHENOMENON

MICHAEL ROUSSELET

People ask me all the time if I'm shocked that *The Room* is still being screened. The answer is no. I'm not shocked; it makes perfect sense to me. I'm incredibly pleased and tickled pinked that it's being shown to new audiences all around the world. What does shock me, however, is the fact that the callback lines and props we created for the first screenings—throwing spoons, wearing ties on heads, bringing roses, throwing footballs, etc.—are still being utilized and expanded upon by complete strangers today. It really hit me when I went to the Ziegfeld Theater's screening of *The Room* in New York in May 2012, and an audience of 1,000 people were shouting out jokes that my friends and I started way back in Los Angeles of July 2003. It was surreal. As a comedian, there was no greater honor than the feeling of 1,000 strangers across the coast reciting your jokes and laughing wildly.

I first discovered *The Room* by accident in June 2003. I saw a trailer for it before a documentary at an art-house theater in Hollywood, and it was the most ridiculous, over-the-top, dramatic, badgering, nonsensical trailer I had ever seen. It told me absolutely nothing, but with so much gusto. It looked hilarious. *Maybe it was a self-aware parody of melodramas,* I thought. But what did I know? I was the only one laughing in the theater. As soon as it left the screen, I forgot about it—that is, until I saw the title on the marquee at a theater by my house. Then it all came rushing back. I had to see it!

Did my friends and I know that what we were getting into at that first initial empty screening back in 2003 would have a real, lasting effect? Good God, no! We thought it would just be your average bad movie, kind of funny here and there, but mostly slow and arduous. Wow! It was far worse than I could have imagined! *The Room* blindsided us. Everything about it was unbelievably hilarious. From the opening line to the last shot, everything was mind-boggling. *The Room* warped our fragile bad movie–loving minds, pushing us to the extreme. It was like a drug. We instantly needed another taste, and we had to tell everyone about it. I called friends on my cellphone before the first screening of *The Room* had even finished, demanding that they come see the next showing.

"Why do I want to pay for a bad film?" they would ask.

"Because it's genius!" I'd reply, as I howled with laughter.

"Wait, is that the movie in the background? Are you calling me from inside the theater?"

"Yes! We are staying for the next screening. If you don't want to pay, I will sneak you in! You have to see this to believe it!"

I suppose the oxymoronic statement "It's so bad, it's brilliant" helped entice friends' curiosity. We stayed in the theater for the next showing, hiding without the ushers seeing us. It's not like they would have been suspicious. I mean, any movie that requires signs to be displayed on the box office window warning, "No tickets will be refunded after twenty minutes of *The Room*"—or that inspires an IMDB review titled "This film is like getting stabbed in the head"—is unlikely to raise employee concern that someone might sneak in to see this piece of garbage. They only started to catch on that something was odd when attendance in that little theater grew from zero to one hundred screaming, shouting teens in the final days.

Why did we spread the word so religiously? I honestly don't know. *The Room* was like a virus. It affected us. We were obsessed. Our enthusiasm was contagious. We couldn't believe that this was a real movie. We couldn't believe Tommy was real! We thought it was a masterfully planned meta-joke. The bad directing, acting, writing, cinematography, editing, production design . . . the film just kept spiraling more and more out of control. Right when you thought *The Room* had reached a plateau of incompetence, it went to a whole other level. It was beautiful. Transcendent. Awe-inspiring. Was Tommy a genius? A new Andy Kaufman? Or just a lucky filmmaker who accidentally did all the wrong moves till everything canceled itself out? It was like a refrigerator film: something an innocent child made that had to be stuck on the fridge for all to see. It was messy but sincere.

We compulsively told every single one of our friends to tell their friends to come see this brilliantly terrible film before it disappeared forever. We even encouraged a buddy system, instructing people to bring another friend. We didn't know how long until *The Room* ended its theatrical run at the Fallbrook Laemmle Theater, but we were damned if our circle of friends was going to miss out. There was no time to waste. Not only did we hit the phones, harassing all of our contacts like militant telemarketers (this was before Facebook and YouTube, and no one of our age really used email), we even passed out *The Room* postcards advertising the screening that Tommy had left around at neighboring malls and drive-thrus. It's amazing (and sad) how much time you have on your hands when you are twenty years old, can't drink, and are stuck in the San Fernando Valley, in the summer, with no job. We became the personal PR team that Tommy never wanted, delivering a message he never approved: "Come see this terrible movie before it's too late!" We might as well have walked around with a sandwich board sign, saying, "The End Is Nigh! Let's Go Eat, Huh!"

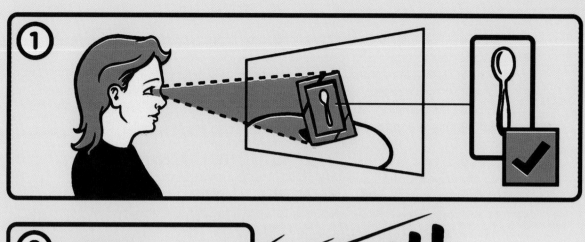

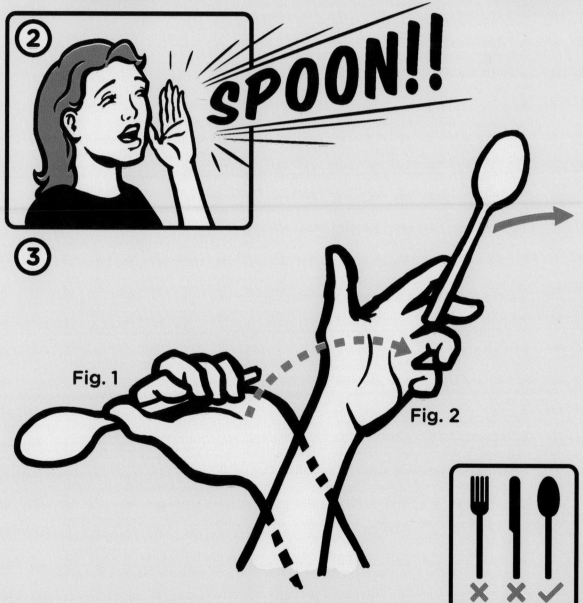

Fig. 1

Fig. 2

Of course, no one outside of our group of friends came to those next three screenings. I guess a couple of unkempt, wide-eyed kids didn't inspire confidence in regular folks that a bad movie was something worth paying for or seeing. But the number of our friends who came to the screenings was growing, and when we were sure that third day was the last day the film would be screening at the theater, we decided to pull out all the stops and give *The Room* its Viking funeral.

"Let's *Rocky Horror* this," I said. "We should bring props!"

We already had the complete control of the theater. No one else was seeing this film but us. Why not? Let's give our friends their money's worth. What could we bring? Footballs were the obvious choice, but we needed something ridiculous—something way out of left field.

As it happened, on my second viewing of *The Room,* when I was manically dissecting the film for scrutiny and foul praise, by chance I noticed something really odd and subtle: a picture of a spoon in a frame. *What? Why?!* Every time it appeared, I would point and scream "Spoon!" to draw attention to it. It got to the point where, on the third screening, people were shouting with me for others to notice. Spoons! "Let's throw plastic spoons!" someone suggested. Sure! So, throwing spoons seemed like a logical choice of accompaniment to this illogical film.

That last night, we took over the theater with one hundred friends, laughing, screaming, and running amok. We dressed up, brought all our props, wore ties on our heads, and shouted in unison our favorite callbacks from the past three screenings. We wanted to make a big, memorable event for our friends before *The Room* disappeared completely. It was an insane and precious experience. By now, the theater manager was baffled and impressed. He knew we were bringing all these people. He even asked me if I wanted a job, because he liked my "initiative." (That Laemmle Theater employee shirt came in handy for screenings years in the future, when I could waltz in for free, even though I had stopped working there.)

Soon, the inevitable happened. *The Room* disappeared. Fortunately, we had achieved our goal of getting a large portion of our friends to see it. They all fell in love with it, of course, and we would quote and talk about nothing else, which in turn made the ones who missed the screenings feel nothing but regret. We tried to track down Tommy, but we could never get a hold of him. We wanted to buy a DVD, but his website seemed like it was trapped in the mid-'90s. We succumbed to using e-mail and signed up for a "fan e-mailing list," sure that nothing would come of it.

Months later, we got an e-mail announcing a private screening at a business center in Beverly Hills. We jumped at it and brought along anyone that could come. Tommy was in attendance, watching us in the back, and it was frightening. Out of respect, we tried not to laugh, but we couldn't hold it in. The film was just too damn funny, even if we'd seen it five times at that point. We were sure Tommy was going to kill us for mocking his dramatic work of art, but he didn't. He didn't say anything, which was even more frightening. It is only recently that we learned that these private screenings were actually "test" screenings. Tommy wanted to know why we were so passionate about his film. I'm sure he was befuddled when tickets sales skyrocketed from zero to a thousand dollars during those last days in July 2003.

A few more business-center screenings came and went, and we kept bringing more friends who had missed out before and now wanted to see what the fanaticism was all about. They too became hypnotized by Tommy's captivating train-wreck charm and were converted to carry our mantra: "Go see *The Room*." It got to the point where we filled up those screenings to maximum capacity, and in 2004 Tommy had to move the film to a larger theater in Hollywood. These were all free screenings, which helped encourage our more hesitant friends to come and finally check out the film. Shortly afterward, Tommy started charging, and people had no choice but to pay for it. He was like a drug pusher, giving us a free taste until we were hooked, and then we had to fork over the dough for our fix. It was a brilliant business strategy. By now, there were so many new faces at those screenings, and even people we didn't know. It became clear that the word was spreading without our help. It was magical. *Oh my God, I wondered, is this going to keep happening?*

Soon, Tommy started doing monthly midnight screenings, and we were obviously obligated to keep bringing more people. It got to the point where we wanted to see if we could sustain this mass hysteria; we had to make sure that we brought as many people as possible to keep it going, and we didn't want it to stop because every screening was new and more hilarious than the last. It was alive. People brought new jokes, ideas, theories, and rumors. There was so much to discuss and expand upon. And if some of the later stragglers didn't really enjoy watching a bad movie, they at least enjoyed the jokes we riffed on, and we enjoyed their horrified screams when Tommy's sex scenes came on.

By the end of 2006, we didn't need to harass friends to come to fill up the theater: it had become a fully self-sustaining enterprise. New fans and curious cinephiles were coming out of the woodwork to see what the deal was with this weird film that people were obsessing over. The Internet started to help carry the load, too, as clips from *The Room* started to show up online to whet people's curiosity. People would even ask me if I had ever heard of *The Room*. It was getting unreal. Then, one day, we realized comedian David Cross was in the theater with us, and we freaked out. *This is legit now! A real comedian is a fan of The Room!* Soon, Cross was followed by Paul Rudd, Jonah Hill, Kristen Bell, David Wain, Bobcat Goldthwait, and Tim & Eric. That's when we knew *The Room* had made it to Hollywood.

In 2008, Clark Collis wrote a huge spread about *The Room* for *Entertainment Weekly*,[1] and with that, it was all over. Overnight, *The Room* became a worldwide phenomenon. It went from one sold-out midnight monthly screening to FIVE simultaneous sold-out screenings in theaters! Tommy booked every screen at the Hollywood Sunset Laemmle to make room for the giant line of roaring fans, and new screenings were popping up all over the country. *The Room* had now secured itself a place in cinema history, and it was entirely our fault.

I still wonder, looking back on that summer day in 2003: *why did we go nuts?* It's just a movie, right? But there was something marvelously unique about *The Room* that a lot of other films don't have, and that's sincerity. It was such a pure, innocent attempt at making a film, almost childlike, even though the film deals with adult themes. Tommy cared so deeply about it, and it was so personal. I guess, deep down, we didn't feel worthy. *The Room* wasn't just a bad movie; it was a brave, honest movie that came from the depths of a man's sad soul. It was as refreshing as it was bewildering, and it would have been a sin to ignore it.

I guess, ultimately, we were attracted to *The Room* because we were fed up with the Hollywood factory of bullshit filmmaking, and we were afraid that something as unique as *The Room* was going to be stepped over and lost forever. We wanted to keep Tommy's dream alive, even if that was just among our own small social circle, but now it looks like we have the help of the entire film-loving world, and that's a beautiful thing. I'm just honored to have been a part of the beginning of this cinematic epidemic.

* * *

Michael Rousselet is a painter, comedian, and filmmaker. He is one of the original members of 5secondfilms.com, which has been featured on *Tosh.0, CNN,* and *Larry King Now,* and in *Spin* and *Wired,* and was named by *Time* as "One of the Top 50 Websites of 2013." Rousselet has been branded "Patient Zero" for starting *The Room* cult phenomenon in July 2003, and has been cited on *CNN* and in *Variety, Entertainment Weekly,* and Greg Sestero's *The Disaster Artist* for his influence. He is currently directing his first feature film, *Dude Bro Party Massacre 3,* a 1980s-style slasher-horror/comedy starring Patton Oswalt and Greg Sestero, to be released in 2015.

4

HOW TO
INFECT OTHERS WITH THE *ROOM* VIRUS

JAMES DURKIN

I first saw Tommy Wiseau's *The Room* on September 10, 2009. Such accuracy might lead you to believe that it was one of the most memorable events in my life, but in all honesty I can only be that precise because I still have the very same copy of it on the hard drive of my computer. The fact that it is still there speaks volumes. For nearly five years, every time I have gone through and deleted old files on this aging laptop, I have hovered my mouse over *The Room*—and then thought better of it. *The Room* abides; it's a permanent fixture, destined to stay until the bitter end. It will probably still be present on this hard drive when I eventually upgrade and send this one to a landfill. And then, who knows? Perhaps it will be found when whatever replaces humanity digs through our wreckage and deciphers our strange way of recording entertainment. Perhaps, one day, this very copy of *The Room* will come to life and beam itself into the eyes of some confused archaeologist, who will congratulate him or herself for finally proving the existence of intelligent mammalian life in this planet's distant past—and then wonder why there is a framed picture of a spoon on the mantelpiece.

While this would constitute the most impressive "passing on" of *The Room* cult I could ever accomplish, far more significant for the purposes of this book would be the time I showed it my friend Ryan Finnigan, a week or so after my initial viewing of it. I'd first encountered the film by reading an article about it in the *Guardian*.[1] The piece, by Steve Rose, covered the film's first UK screening following its growing cult status is the US, and was titled, "Is this the worst movie ever made?"—which was probably the most appealing headline ever written (to me, at least). Rose also invoked the works of Ed Wood and R. Kelly, two other artists whose works had entertained me.

After reading this article, I knew two things: I had to see this film, and I had to show it to Ryan. He and I had met on the film studies degree course at Sheffield Hallam University, and we were both avid fans of cinema. With time on our hands and access to the university's film library, we have watched a lot of films together over the years. Perhaps exposure to so much quality cinema eventually inoculated our minds against high culture; I'm not sure, but at some juncture we started to become more interested in bad films than good ones. It's hard to say exactly why some

films are more artistically successful than others, and it is even harder when there is at least some form of aesthetics that can be agreed on. It may be clear on so many levels that *Tokyo Story* is a much better film than *Basket Case,* but I know which one I would rather re-watch, and which one I have fonder memories of.

The action film *Crank* may have been the tipping point. It was a film we idolized on the strength of its trailer, which showed Jason Statham playing a hit man with only hours to live and scores to settle, and hit just the right tone of ridiculousness for us. It was all we talked about once the disappointing feature that followed it, *Snakes on a Plane,* had ended. We watched the trailer online, over and over again, and our enthusiasm for it far outstripped that of other, more worthy cinema. When it came out, the film was entertaining and did not disappoint, yet I think that first glimpse of the trailer was the high point.

From then on, we were more likely to watch a Troma movie than sit through a Tarkovsky, and we found that introducing a friend to a bad film was far more fun than sitting them down to a good one. A real enthusiasm for terrible cinema is characterized by excitement. Discovering something incomprehensibly bad and sharing it with others is far more exciting and infectious an experience than sitting down to a three-star run-of-the-mill DVD, now that mainstream cinema is screen-tested into a sea of watchable blandness. There's also an element of sadism in inflicting the viewing pain on others, or a catharsis in passing it on, in the style of the tape from *Ringu.*

Bad cinema can be a uniting force much more so than great cinema, because there is so much more to say about it that's fun. Of course, the real joy isn't just recommending a film to someone; it's sitting down and watching it with them. If you share the same sense of humor, a bad film provides endless material to riff on, getting the creative juices flowing much more than praising a good film would. And, if you talk over it, people don't give you funny looks.

So, after tracking down and watching a copy of *The Room,* I knew that I wanted to share it. This truly was one of the worst films I had ever seen . . . and yet it was watchable. It had seemingly been written and directed by some kind of a madman and edited by a comedic genius who seemed to have it in for him. I must have raved about it, as Ryan traveled to another city just to see it. The film became even funnier on that shared viewing, and elements of the film soon entered our collective vernacular—or, at least, that's the idea!

I was far from the first to discover the film, but in introducing the film to Ryan, I played a small part in passing on the strange fascination of *The Room,* eventually to a room full of hundreds of strangers at a screening he hosted—hundreds of strangers who all hopefully went out and spread the word themselves. The film is something that almost instantly captivates people even when you're simply telling them about it, and their morbid fascination grows as they see it. *The Room* is an organic, viral epidemic of exponential growth, and the word-of-mouth community that has grown out of that, again, sets it apart from the films that we are "told" to watch. If I ever experience guilt when watching *The Room* yet again, when I could be watching something more conventionally worthy, I'll think of this.

* * *

James Durkin is a twenty-nine-year-old writer. Having studied for a degree in film studies at Sheffield Hallam University, he went on to study at the University of Leeds, graduating with an MA in writing for performance and publication in 2010. A regular contributing scriptwriter for the *Doctor Who Audio Dramas* website, he was also shortlisted in 2013 for Sheffield Theatres' *20 Tiny Plays about Sheffield,* and is TV Editor for [SIC] Blog, while also working with [SIC] as a screenwriter and production assistant. When he isn't frantically working on scripts, James works as a clerical assistant, and currently lives in Sheffield with his partner Ruth and Bobbi the cat.

5

HOW TO
TALK TO YOUR FRIENDS ABOUT
BECOMING A FAN OF *THE ROOM*
STEVE HEISLER

Yes, that is really how it ends. It's been ninety-nine minutes. I know, right? It feels like you've been watching forever. You probably have a lot of questions. What kind of drugs did Denny take? Who was that guy at the end who talked about "sitting on an atomic bomb about to go off," and how was it that he was such good friends with Lisa all of a sudden? Why? And so forth.

Wondering and obsessing are both a natural part of the process. You have just seen *The Room,* and have been rocked by the passion of Tennessee Williams and the droopy tuxedoed face of success. You are likely to be seriously confused. But I cannot stress enough: no matter how many questions you may have, *RESIST THE TEMPTATION TO ASK ALL OF THOSE QUESTIONS ALL AT ONCE.* Are you really prepared to become that person who won't stop talking about how their new Soda Stream has, like, completely changed their life? Just put *The Room* in place of the Soda Stream. Or Jesus. The last thing you want to do is scare anyone away with your terrifyingly real theories about Lisa's jingoistic pizza order (half Canadian bacon and pineapple, half artichoke and pesto, light on the cheese).

After I saw *The Room* for the first time, all I wanted to do was find out if all the bat-shit crazy things I had just seen came from delusions of grandeur, or just delusions. Basically, I needed to know if Tommy Wiseau had any self-awareness whatsoever in creating his masterpiece, and the pursuit was all-consuming. I manufactured a flimsy excuse to interview him for the *A. V. Club* and dug deep into the film's head-scratching mythology—most notably, where the fuck could Tommy Wiseau possibly be from? Poland? Russia? France? New Orleans? The Cheesecake Factory? I published lots of articles about roses and such because I refused to spend any of my days not talking about, writing about, or being without *The Room.*

Around the time I snagged Greg Sestero—aka best friend Mark—for an interview, my editor told me to shut the fuck up. He was likely speaking for most of my friends, as well as the vast majority of polite society. I had seen something in *The Room* that I could not un-see, and I'm not just talking about Tommy's cottage-cheese butt cheeks. I saw unfiltered ambition. A movie that not only claimed to have it all and then did, but that went so far out of its way to make a statement about Lisa's feminine evil that it must have gotten lost, because it decided to have not one but TWO scenes about a character's underwear—and we never saw that person again. Also, the third sex scene uses literally the exact same footage as the first one. I went frame by frame.

Had I heeded the following tips, perhaps I wouldn't be here today, writing a helpful guide about how not to be the kind of guy who has to write a helpful guide because his friends and loved ones just don't understand, man. But to quote the great Tommy Wiseau, "That is personal. Anyway, how's your sex life?" As in: yes, there is a way to be tactful about sharing your newfound blind love.

"You never get a second chance to make a first impression" is the kind of clichéd bullshit you have to remember when broaching the subject with your friends, because thanks to hipster stereotypes, bad movies have become a very prevalent part of stereotypical hipster culture. Stereotypical hipsters love doing things they hate. Now, since it's not cool in stereotypical hipster culture to conform to popular opinion, the ironic viewing of terrible movies is scoffed at. So, to get your friends to even pay attention, you have to say more than just, "It's sooooooo bad."

I have a little elevator speech I've practiced that seems to get the job done nicely:

> **The Room** is an amazing movie. It's obviously very horrible, but it's horrible in such an over-the-top way that you can't believe what you're watching actually exists. It's kind of about a guy whose fiancée cheats on him with his best friend, but there's also a character who says she has breast cancer once and then they never mention it again. There's a random drug dealer scene on a roof—which, by the way, they green-screened. Oh yeah, the lead in the movie is this vaguely Eastern European guy named Tommy Wiseau, who looks like what would happen if you took a He-Man action figure and melted it in the microwave for a few seconds. AND IT COST $6 MILLION TO MAKE.

If they are not even the least bit intrigued after all that, give up. This person is a lost cause, but more importantly they can go fuck themselves.

"You have to see it to believe it" is also something that is true in the case of *The Room.* Offer to host a viewing party. Nothing says "Please watch this movie" like you saying those exact words and then setting a date. I've found that ten-to-twelve people is the sweet spot, with roughly a third being folks who've already seen the movie, and two-thirds who

The Room Viewing Party:
Guidelines For Hosting

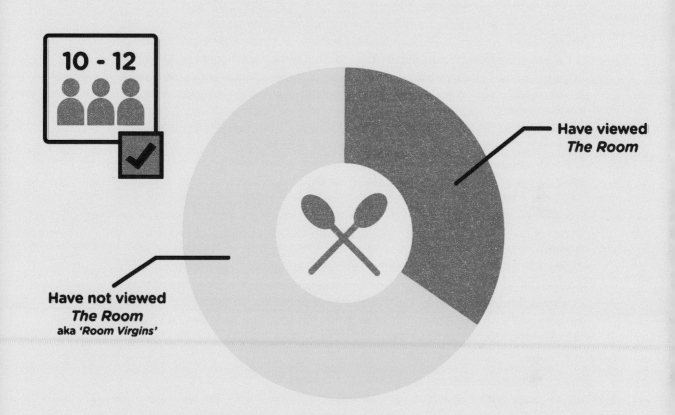

10 - 12

Have viewed
The Room

Have not viewed
The Room
aka 'Room Virgins'

haven't. It's just the right amount of people to knowingly shrug when a newbie hears their first "Oh hai, Mark."

Get everyone drunk and high.

Now, pay attention, because this is the really important part that will guarantee you've made *Room* friends for life. Just like you, they will have a million questions throughout the movie. Do NOT—I repeat, *DO NOT*—answer any of them. I know that is a hard impulse to stifle, but stifle it you must. Trust me. They will keep watching, mouth agape, genitalia shriveling into nonexistence, at the film's sheer boner-killing potential, trying to add up this violently illogical film for themselves. After ninety-nine minutes, the credits will roll, and everyone will turn to you, now the Christ-like figure Tommy Wiseau could never be. Don't give them everything at once. Make them work for it.

"Yes, that is really how it ends."

* * *

Steve Heisler is a New York–based comedy journalist who's written for *Rolling Stone,* the *A. V. Club, Variety, Fast Company,* and *New York Magazine.* He is also a die-hard comedy nerd who has worked for the Just for Laughs festival, and is more than a little obsessed with that one scene in *The Room* where Denny jumps into the bed.

6

HOW TO
WATCH *THE ROOM* IF YOU'RE JULIETTE DANIELLE
JULIETTE DANIELLE

My first uncensored thought when asked to write this chapter involved a string of negative expletives. After all, I don't watch *The Room* anymore. Ever. EVER.

When I tell *Room*-virgin friends and family that I won't watch the film, they almost always react with an emphatic, "WHY NOT?" After all, I AM the star of a feature-length film. That's, like, amazing. Right?!

For those who have actually seen the movie and given it more than just a passing thought, I believe it is pretty obvious why the viewing experience for me is incredibly unique. Robyn Paris, who played Michelle, sometimes dons a wig and goes to screenings with her friends. I was originally cast to play Michelle. There are certainly days I wish I could trade places with her. She can truly laugh at the film and enjoy it for what it is. She can separate herself from it. In fact, I think most of the cast members can. I guess if anyone should be embarrassed, other than me, it would be Tommy. But *The Room* is Tommy's baby. His masterpiece. He loves the notoriety and attention. And he deserves it.

I cannot relate my experience as a lead actress with Whitney Moore in *Birdemic: Shock and Terror* or Margo Prey in *Troll 2.* No one that I know of has experienced the same degree of humiliation I did on that fateful premiere night of *The Room,* which was my first viewing. I had never seen it before the premiere. Big mistake.

The fact is, I have seen the movie in its entirety less than a handful of times. I will happily watch montage and mash-up clips on the Internet, and can laugh at the fully clothed Lisa tributes on YouTube. But for me to be able to watch the film through again, in a packed theater, and not be negatively affected, would require me to be heavily sedated or completely devoid of human emotion all together. As Goldie Hawn's Elise states so perfectly in *The First Wives Club,* "You think that because I'm a movie star I don't have feelings. Well, you're wrong. I'm an actress. I've got all of them!" I'm quite a sensitive little bug. I guess God didn't want me to have thick skin, because, try as I might, I cannot grow it.

My mother loves *The Room.* As weird as that is, she has consistently loved it in a non-ironic way since the first time she watched it. God bless that woman. She laughs every time I say, "I don't want to talk about it." (Turns out that is a really useful line that I consistently deploy in real life.)

My entire family has been instructed not to watch *The Room*. My husband has never watched the film—and, with any luck, he never will. My friends have made their own decisions about whether they want to watch it or not. When I joined my church a few years ago, I had to have the difficult discussion with my pastor as to why he shouldn't bring his wife to one of the midnight screenings. When I explained that I'm naked for the majority of the movie, he kept a poker face and just said, "OK then." He is now a subscriber to my fully clothed YouTube channel. Bless his heart.

I remember my father calling me a few years ago and telling me he was excited to watch *The Room* on Comedy Central, which was an April Fools' programming tradition for a few years. I told him he would probably regret it, but I gave him my blessing anyway. He seemed determined. He was sure that, since it would be edited for television, it would be OK to watch. The next day, I received an email from him that said only the following:

> **"Honey, I just wanted you to know I turned it off as soon as the black boxes came on."**

But this is a book about watching and enjoying *The Room,* not avoiding it. So, let me put my thinking cap on and ponder the perfect situation that would allow me to experience the film. One. More. Time.

My Fantasy Theater Viewing Experience

Step 1: Cut out all the love scenes. The movie is now the perfect length to submit to a short film festival. Put Tommy's butt in the blooper reel at the end. Everyone wins. All the laughs . . . none of the panic attacks!

Step 2: Give my neck bulge its own dialogue. And, while we are adding sound effects, let's add an actual "BOOP" sound every time Claudette/Carolyn touches my nose, and CGI an atomic bomb exploding at the Golden Gate Bridge during one of those epic camera pans.

Step 3: Hire WWE's the Shield, aka the "Hounds of Justice," to police any and all body-snark comments from the audience. Any creative commentary directed toward my actual character will be high-fived, and given a large chocolate cupcake to eat with a plastic spoon.

Step 4:   Down a glass of wine to ease my suffering, as I will soon be watching a twenty-year-old me attempt to convey complex internal emotions by simply wrinkling up my face and delivering the same ridiculous lines again and again, with a mildly disgusted look.

Step 5:   During the Q&A before the screening, pour a second glass of wine to help me ignore that jerk in the back row who asks me, for the 500th time, "What's it like to get your belly button $^&#ed?" Breathe. Pour a third glass of wine. (I wish I had that special talent Greg Sestero has that allows him to successfully deflect and humorously quip a response to every uncomfortable question asked of him during these Q&As. Or, that SUPERPOWER Tommy has that helps him to deliver an answer in the form of an incoherent twenty-minute speech, while saying absolutely nothing tangible, and without any relation to the original question—and yet the fans LOVE IT anyway. He is a master. I am in awe.)

Step 6:   Ignore every urge to run out of the theater in shame. As the movie plays, pull out a flask of wine and contemplate how boring my life would have been without *The Room.* Cry a little. Laugh a little. Earn one of those large chocolate cupcakes by shouting at the screen myself.
"What KIND of money?" Wait a minute. That feels good. Yeah!
"Because I'm a woman!"
"BOOP!"

Step 7:   Quick, someone get me a box of spoons! This IS fun!
"SPOON!"
throw
Repeat.
Oh wait, it's over? Sigh. This movie IS short without all those love scenes.

Step 8:   Hold on to the movie seats as I make my way toward the aisle. I've lost count of how much wine I've had, and I'm a lightweight these days.

Step 9: Take photos and sign autographs with our awesome fans after the screening. Who cares if my hair is a mess, my mascara has run down my cheeks, and I smell like a winery? My cats will always love me, and there are no plans for a sequel to *The Room*. Let a sense of well being return to my body.

Step 10: Never repeat again.

There! That was quite freeing!

I sincerely hope everyone reading this book understands that I appreciate the experience and the journey *The Room* has taken me on over these many years. I truly love our fans—our "Roomies." They are one of a kind. I hope they keep having fun with friends at midnight screenings, quoting lines, sharing inside jokes—and, of course, bringing more Roomies into this phenomenal circle of insanity.

* * *

Behind Lisa, the ruthless, self-centered femme fatale of *The Room,* lies the charming and sweet Texan actress Juliette Danielle. Having shied away from the attention that *The Room* brought to her door, she was eventually able to embrace the film and rediscover the confidence to return to performing, both in acting and stand-up comedy. A cat-rescue volunteer, keen wrestling fan, and able *Minecraft* player, she's the three-dimensional lady behind the one-dimensional Lisa.

PART TWO

"COMPREHENSION"

ANALYSIS AND INTERVIEWS

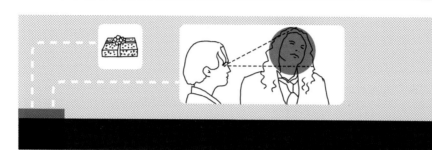

0:00:00–0:09:04

From its opening shot, a slow pan down from an idyllic blue sky to the iconic Golden Gate Bridge, *The Room* labors to establish its setting, San Francisco. Imagery of landmarks such as Alcatraz, the Palace of Fine Arts, and the famed sloping streets instantly evokes the city's spectacular cinematic lineage, with films such as *Bullitt, Dirty Harry, The Maltese Falcon,* and *Vertigo* all burned into our collective conscious. Such a heavy focus on location insinuates that *The Room's* atmosphere will be heavily influenced by San Francisco's status as a leading cultural and financial center in California, yet beyond these bland establishing shots, nothing of the city's culture is represented at all. According to a United States census taken just three years before *The Room's* release, San Francisco had a minority-majority population, a third of it Asian,[1] yet not a single non-white face appears throughout the film. Why go to such lengths to establish a film's location if it is to have no influence on the story?

Consider the geography of John Ford's 1956 film *The Searchers,* one of the most beautifully shot American movies of the 1950s. John Wayne's Ethan Edwards traverses Utah's Monument Valley in his quest to find his niece, with the location not only playing its part in the film's aesthetics but also fulfilling a less obvious role as the film's secret antagonist. The tough, rugged, and majestic landscape serves as more of a threat to Edwards than any Native American weaponry, ready to punish those who don't respect it. The harshness of the environment not only serves to highlight the inner toughness of the characters in surviving it, but also provides a palpable, consistent danger to them. This prominence of location creates a conscious and subconscious atmosphere that gives the characters a grit and nobility that, in lesser hands, would likely have been conveyed through exposition. In *The Room,* the prominence of location serves as nothing more than competently shot yet consistently overused eye candy; it comes as the result of the director's inability to think of any other way to start his film, rather than as an attempt to ground his characters in reality.

As the director's credit fades in to a shot of an apartment, we meet the first of the characters with whose lives we will become so indelibly linked during the following ninety-nine minutes. The camera pans across from a window, daylight streaming brightly through, and stops on a door that opens to let in our hero, Tommy Wis—err, Johnny. We're never told Johnny's surname, though given the phonetic similarity, and the stench of autobiography that clings to the film throughout, it wouldn't be too wild a guess to assume that it at least rhymes with Wiseau. Regardless, this entrance serves as the blueprint for every entrance for the remainder of the film: awkward, badly staged, and unnatural. Johnny staggers through the door, almost lost in the ill-fitting suit that seems to be his only clothing, apart from his gym wear, and emits his infamous catchphrase: "Hi/Oh hai, [name]."

The camera cuts to Lisa—the plainest of femme fatales—who is sitting on the sofa. Literally sitting on the sofa—there's no book to be read, no music or television playing, not even a cup of coffee steaming on the table before her. She is a loyal dog at the door, sat in stasis, awaiting Johnny's appearance to bring her to life, like a video-game enemy that doesn't become activated until the playable character comes within a certain distance. This returns us to the issue of the film's inability to create any tangible sense of reality outside the edge of its frames, demonstrating Wiseau's genuine misunderstanding of what makes a film a film. (It's not surprising that a film so clearly plagued by a feeling of staginess started

life as a script for a stage play. Stage and screen have different strengths and weaknesses, and Wiseau doesn't seem to fully comprehend either.)

Without saying a word, Lisa stands and takes one step toward Johnny before the camera cuts straight back to him, affording her the shortest possible character-establishing shot. Johnny has something for her, and he's hiding it behind his back. Lisa, whose awkward tugs at her blue top make us begin to wonder whether anyone in this film can dress themselves properly, moves toward Johnny and makes a grab for whatever he's hiding, as he playfully swings side-to-side to keep it out of her reach.

"What is it?" Lisa asks, scrunching up her face.

"Just a little something," Johnny replies, seemingly throwing his voice, thanks to a painfully miscued overdub. Eventually, Johnny hands over a gaudily wrapped leopard-skin box, which Lisa clumsily opens to reveal a red dress, all the while under the vacant stare of her beloved.

"Johnny, it's beautiful," Lisa coos. "Can I try it on now?"

"Sure, of course. It's yours," he slurs in response, the very essence of disinterest. Lisa disappears upstairs to try on the dress, and we fade to her coming back down.

A trill of a harp sound alerts us to the staggering beauty we are about to see, but instead we get Lisa. Johnny's voice-throwing perfects itself here, his "Wow, you look so sexy Lisa" sounding like it has come from, well, anywhere other than where he is actually sitting. Lisa gives him a twirl, which we almost completely miss due to the film inexplicably cutting to a close-up of her face, before quickly cutting back again, with Wiseau having realized that any close-up of Lisa means Johnny *isn't actually on screen* for that particular moment. Johnny makes it three-for-three with his third attempt at speaking—"I would do anything for my girl"—a line so hopelessly dubbed as to create the impression that the only place it could have come from is the very depths of hell. (As a side-note, I'm going to stop mentioning the ADR issues in the film from this point on, as they are so prominent throughout that it would be as time-consuming, and frustrating, as individually cataloguing each use of the word "the.")

The camera cuts to the door just in time to catch it opening for our first supporting character, Denny. Wiseau does well here as he manages to prepare us for the bizarre, nonsensical Denny by giving him a suitably bizarre, nonsensical introduction: stepping in as if from a standing position, and without his hand on the doorknob, it's as though Denny has willed the door open with his mind. Maybe Denny has psychic powers—is he an idiot savant, rather than just an idiot? Given that, without this secret, Denny's entire existence is solely to provide characters a point of exposition to extol Johnny's kindness, it's better to think of him as a subconscious hint to a mystical world running concurrently alongside the film's primary narrative.

"Hey, guys," says Denny, imaginatively. Lisa just looks at him before

Johnny returns his bullet in this battle of wits: "Hey, Denny." We are then afforded a pointless shot of Denny walking across the room to enter the conversation, because apparently there are only two positions from which the cameras can actually shoot, and Denny isn't in the one from which we can see every character.

Straightaway, Denny comments on Lisa's attractiveness—a recurring theme, as if Wiseau is trying to trick the audience into believing he has landed an A-list Hollywood beauty for the role—before, in an incredibly ham-fisted attempt to showcase the character's social awkwardness, rudely enquiring as to how much her new dress cost. Ignoring this, Johnny stands up and says, "Nice to see you, Denny," before euphemistically telling Lisa, "I'm going to take a nap." It seems strange to try to introduce one character's social awkwardness through an innocuous line of dialogue about money and then, five seconds later, have one of your supposedly well-adjusted characters whisk away his fiancée for sex within a minute of another character entering his home. Yet that's the Wiseau logic with which we will become familiar soon enough.

Laughing off Denny's request to come with them, Johnny departs, taking Lisa with him. We cut to an incredibly badly framed and poorly focused shot of the pair disappearing up the spiral staircase before returning to Denny. As he eavesdrops on the banal conversation upstairs, Denny reaches down to pluck up an apple, greedily taking a bite out of it. The most obvious symbolism associated with apples is that of temptation, though there is also a link to a loss of innocence. Could the apple be seen to represent Denny's forbidden lust for Lisa? Does the fact he has taken a bite show his readiness to act upon that lust and ruin his innocence? We can easily attach any meaning we like upon the apple, but judging by the depth of subtext in the rest of the film, we should instead come to the safe assumption that Denny is hungry. Either way, the suitably emboldened Denny rushes upstairs for . . . well, I'm not sure exactly. Having already made us aware of his underlying psychopathic nature with his inquiry about the cost of a dress, we could guess that Denny's lack of social skills mean he's completely unaware of what Johnny and Lisa are up to, but it seems more likely he either wants to (a) prevent them having sex out of jealousy, or (b) have a threesome.

Upstairs, Johnny and Lisa are having a playful pillow fight, with Johnny's delightfully out-of-place and half-hearted "peeeuuuwww" sounding like the kind of noise a bored parent makes when trying to "land the airplane" during their child's lunchtime. Suddenly, Denny surprises us by jumping into the fray from out of nowhere . . . except, he doesn't, a pointless cutaway shot shows Denny arriving at the top of the stairs, denying us even that small surprise. The pillow fight itself is disappointingly half-hearted; it feels more like a rehearsal than anything remotely close to the passion and romance that the dialogue is trying so hard to convince us is present in this particular relationship. After several weak, uncoordinated swings of the pillow, Denny is tickled in a close-up so close that it's difficult to tell what's actually going on. Eventually, he's forced to the floor, from where he looks up at love's young dream, lying side by side.

"Don't you have something else to do?" Johnny asks, to which Denny replies, "I just like to watch you guys," in a not-at-all-creepy-manner. It's so reminiscent of Chance from *Being There* that we can't help but wish that this is a reference to the Peter Sellers role. Alas, we know it's not. Denny's just scary.

Denny leaves to do his homework, and we settle down to a sex scene that is, in its own way, infinitely more unsettling than the butter-buggery in *Last Tango in Paris.* As the horrible, generic R&B music kicks in, we are instantly dragged out of the scene by jarring shifts in atmosphere and continuity, such as Johnny's suit jacket being back on now, despite his having removed it for the pillow fight. The enraptured pair seem to have stopped halfway through foreplay and decided, "This really isn't the right atmosphere, let's take five minutes to get everything set up," as strategically placed soft lighting and candles have appeared from nowhere to provide a clichéd "film-sex" mood, robbing the scene of any notion of romantic spontaneity—and again establishing the film's lack of anything inherently cinematic. The sex scene itself is pure exploitation. There is an incredible amount of dubbed grunting and moaning, a worrying number of shots of Johnny's butt, and a ridiculous number of soft-focus shots through doily curtains and . . . is that rain, or just more tacky décor? Perhaps the oddest aspect of the scene is the way that Johnny seems to be thrusting into Lisa's abdomen rather than his, ahem, intended target.

While the scene ostensibly does little more than highlight the lack of any chemistry—sexual or otherwise—between the two leads, it does actually lead into the start of the film's central conflict. After the sex is mercifully over—and it's a *long* three minutes and twelve seconds—Lisa turns to Johnny. She seems ready to talk, but the lovemaking session was all too vigorous for Johnny who, being a man, is already falling asleep. Sighing in disappointment, she turns off the light before turning back to him, snorting an implied, derisive, "Is that all you got, Johnny Boy?" before embracing him as we fade to black.

LISA
JULIETTE DANIELLE

INTERVIEW

Oh hai, Juliette! What are your prevalent feelings about *The Room* now?
Oh hai, right back at you! My prevalent feeling at the moment is thank GOD some of those memories from the shoot are starting to get fuzzy. Just kidding. I think it's great that something I was a part of has been culturally relevant for so long.

Could you see a future for *The Room* while you were on set, and did you think you'd be still talking about it ten years later?
Oh, heck no. I never thought anyone would see it. But I underestimated Tommy. No one should do that, ever.

What was your acting background, prior to *The Room*? Tell me a little bit about getting involved with the project, and your initial feelings about it . . .
I had practically no acting background. I did school plays when I was very young, and had started taking some acting classes, but it was very new. I was very green. My initial thoughts? "OH MY GOD! I'M IN A MOVIE!!!! I need to call . . . EVERYBODY!!!!"

In *The Disaster Artist,* Greg Sestero relates that you were a very positive presence on set. How did you manage to keep a positive mind-set when it sounds as though many other people were losing their patience and/or sanity?
Greg is a sweetheart. He was actually one of the things that kept me going, day to day. He's a good friend to have, and has a great sense of humor. And I seriously love acting. I was having a great time—except for those times when I wasn't having a great time.

In that sense, it might be fair to say you were working with an "insensitive" director and having to deal with difficult situations. How would you act differently now?

Tommy is intense and eccentric, yes, but he's a nice guy. He was under a lot of pressure, I'm sure. Of course, there were some difficult situations, and I would certainly handle things differently now. I learned how to speak up for myself and still be respectful. Age has a lot to do with it. I found my "sense of self" very late in life.

I'm interested to know how you feel about Lisa, and how you approached the character. By all accounts, you're a happy, well-liked person, and Lisa is just so conniving and mean! Did you enjoy playing a wicked character?

Oh, God, I wish I could go back and play her again. She would have so many more layers. At the time of shooting, I didn't have a lot of life experience to draw from. I LOVE playing characters different from myself. That's the fun of acting.

Despite seemingly being a frustrating time, *The Room* must have been a lot of fun to work on as well. Have you got any favorite memories of the shoot and how would you describe your fellow cast and crew?

The cast were terrific. We didn't have trailers, so we hung out a lot. All of us were on set most of the time. We'd listen to Carolyn Minnott [Claudette] tell stories, watch Tommy's antics from afar, and talk about how on earth we would deliver our crazy lines.

What has life been like after *The Room*? It seems to me that you probably had a lot more to process after the film's release than anyone else. Lisa is not only an unlikeable character, but also a lot of the attention directed toward her at screenings can be pretty cruel . . .

I'm perfectly aware of how bad it gets in screenings. It's one of the reasons I never go into the theater while it is playing anymore. Sometimes I feel pretty isolated in this respect. Most of the other cast members could laugh at the experience pretty early on. It took me years. The toll it took on my body image was harsh. I hid. But over time it became less painful. I had more conversations with people who drew so much joy from the film. I began to concentrate on that and interact with my fans. So, all in all, I'm pretty OK with it. It's just every now and then, a fan will get the chance to ask me any question they want, and they will ask something like, "What's it like to have Tommy f*** your hip?" I mean, seriously, how do you even answer that question? One begins to see why Tommy is so evasive with questioning.

On the flip side, *The Room* is an international phenomenon, and you must have met some great fans over the years . . .

I am so happy I get a chance to make sure all our fans know how much we love and appreciate them. When someone posts a photo on my Facebook fan page of them dressed up as Lisa, with a big smile on their faces, my heart soars. Something I was a part of brings friends together on a regular basis, gives them an excuse to dress up, and fuels inside jokes. How cool is that? I credit my fans with my decision to return from the murky shadows of hiding.

It seems as though, despite laughing at the film, no one actually dislikes *The Room* or anyone in it. What is it that you think makes it so endearing?

Oh, there are some people that dislike *The Room*. They are the people that didn't have a friend introduce them to it. They ordered it on Netflix one day and had no idea what was in store for them. I LOVE to read those reviews, actually. They are seriously pissed. But for the ones that love it, and keep loving it, screening after screening . . . you have to credit Tommy. He's so accessible to fans. He keeps the love going.

Do you ever regret doing *The Room*? One thing that occurred to me in seeing your stand-up comedy is that, at the very least, it must have made you ready to face anything!

Of course I do, but not all the time. So that's an improvement. My stand-up comedy is pretty new. I'm still finding myself. I can tell you, though, that I get so terrified before going up. Stage fright is the worst!

Would you ever act in another Tommy Wiseau project?

Although working with Tommy is most likely a once-in-a-lifetime experience . . . I'd definitely work with him again. How fun would that be? But I don't think he's going to ask.

We fade in to the shrill buzz of an alarm clock that's in its rightful position: on the floor, next to Johnny's bed. Maybe the rigorous sex session the night before knocked it to the ground. An arm snakes down to lift it up, and we see Johnny playing with the buttons on the side. The buzzing doesn't stop, however, until Johnny drops the alarm clock on the floor—or at least that's what the FAR-too-loud-in-the-mix Foley effect suggests. I guess Johnny has one of those motion-sensor alarm clocks that were all the rage in 2003; either that, or the sound engineer doesn't know how alarm clocks work. Another issue with Johnny's alarm clock is that it's set for twenty-eight minutes past the hour. Who sets their alarm clock for such a specific time? Johnny is clearly very exact about how long he needs to get ready for work.

Without moving his mouth, Johnny lets out a groan and slumps back into bed before getting up, taking a deep smell of a rose from his bedside table, and placing it next to the sleeping Lisa. We are now awarded a glorious shot of Wiseau's chiseled ass as he walks to the bathroom, closing the door behind him, before fading to Lisa playing with the rose left beside her, a satisfied look on her face. Johnny being the kind of man who keeps his suits in the bathroom, he re-enters the bedroom.

"Did you like last night?" he asks. "Yes, I did," Lisa replies. Johnny laughs happily.

Words cannot describe how successfully this film turns what is intended as a romantic moment into a seedy, uncomfortable exchange. On the set of *Star Wars,* Harrison Ford famously told George Lucas, "George, you can type this shit, but you sure as hell can't say it."[1] I defy anyone to find any Han Solo line—even one about Parsecs and Kessel Runs—that seems less natural and human than the way Johnny talks to Lisa here.

Their morning routine complete, Johnny leaves for work as Lisa naps contentedly. Now, I'm assuming anyone reading this will have already seen *The Room,* so to say that the main thrust of the story concerns Lisa having an affair is not exactly a spoiler. This scene, however, makes absolutely no sense in the context of the next five minutes. Every aspect of what follows is built on Lisa's dissatisfaction in her relationship, and yet here there is no build up to it—she looks genuinely blissful, even in the moments when Johnny cannot see her. It's just bad filmmaking/acting/everything *not* to use Lisa's private moments to begin to sow the seeds of doubt in this relationship. A character's private moments are the ones that define their motivation and provide the drama; the greatest tension in cinema often stems from knowing something that the characters don't, and trying to will what we know onto them is key in creating that emotional connection. Think of the moment in Bryan Singer's *The Usual Suspects,* when Verbal Kint is waiting in Agent Kujan's office, nonchalantly looking around the office to alleviate his boredom until the agent arrives; the ending reveals that he was actually using the time to formulate his alibi. Using a character's private moments as a way to define them is filmmaking at its very best, with this example allowing Kevin Spacey to show his character's cunning and quick thinking, subtly betraying his apparently naïve exterior. Admittedly, this is something the viewer might only realize through a second or third viewing, but the fact holds that, regardless of how many times you watch it, there is nothing in the opening ten minutes of *The Room,* save for Lisa's derisive snort, to imply that her relationship with Johnny is anything other than perfectly functional. It makes the evolution into the following ten minutes unnatural, unbelievable, and improbable. And that, really, is *The Room* in three words.

Although the location remains the same, we cut to the living room via an establishing shot of Johnny's townhouse. Lisa—now with noticeably shorter hair—walks over to the door, opening it to introduce us to her mother, Claudette. Straightaway, Claudette is fussing over Lisa, taking her over to the couch for an amateur counseling session. Lisa tries to change the subject before finally caving in, and admitting, "I don't love him anymore." Somehow—don't ask me how—the apocalypse doesn't break out at this revelation, and the scene continues.

Claudette seems strangely uninterested, considering her previous concern about what is, in all honesty, an important event in her daughter's life. "Why don't you love him? Tell me," she asks, more out of social convention than any genuine interest. Lisa searches deep inside for the answer and—ignoring the plethora of reasons we've already been shown as to why no woman could ever love Johnny—she plumps for, "He's so . . . boring." I'd have gone for the belly-button sex fetish, myself, but it's hard not to disagree.

"Well, you've known him for over five years," Claudette replies. Over five years—wow. Our thoughts turn to just how many times Lisa must have heard Johnny say "Oh hai" during that time. The camera hangs awkwardly on Lisa, with Juliette Danielle clearly given no direction on how to react or behave in front of it, as Claudette reels off a list of reasons why Lisa can't leave Johnny. It's an increasingly desperate eulogy:

> He supports you. He provides for you. You can't support yourself. He's a wonderful man. He loves you very much. His position is very secure. He plans to buy you a house. He bought you a car. He bought you a ring. He bought you clothes—whatever you wanted. And now you want to dump him. That's not right. I've always thought of him as my son-in-law. You should marry Johnny. He would be good for you.

For cinemagoers in 1970, love meant never having to say you're sorry. Here, in 2003, it apparently means, "He does everything for you. Respect him." The whole scene reeks of Wiseau's twisted ideology of what makes a strong relationship. Every single aspect of Claudette's eulogy is focused on materialism; there's no consideration of Lisa's emotional or spiritual needs. This vicarious self-defense comes off as teenage poetry of the highest order—all delusions of grandeur and self-justification against understandable disquiet. Furthermore, instead of being portrayed as a woman to be desired, Lisa becomes nothing more than a parasite in a symbiotic relationship. Claudette makes it sound as if Lisa would be doing Johnny a favor by leaving.

The scene peters out with a directionless exchange about how no one listens to Claudette before she announces she has to go, kick-starting the film's befuddling trope of having characters enter a scene, deliver ninety seconds of exposition, and then suddenly remember that they have an important appointment they need to be getting to. As we leave the scene, special attention must go to the cameraman who, in every single close-up of the conversation, fails to frame the actresses properly. To paraphrase Jim Gordon at the end of *The Dark Knight,* it was the camerawork the scene deserved, but not the camerawork it needed.

Another scene, another fade-in, as Lisa picks up the phone. Again, the bridge between scenes is incredibly unnatural. During the fade, she's sitting down, staring into space, and then she turns to pick up the phone and dial, in a moment so obviously staged that your mind almost fills in Wiseau shouting "Action" and Juliette Danielle starting into what passes for acting. Upon watching the final edit, you wonder, *How did Wiseau not notice how distracting this staging is?*

A new character, Mark, answers and Lisa addresses him with the words, "Hey, baby. How're you doing?" This creates some confusion— why would she call him "baby"? Are they having an affair? Mark doesn't so much as bat an eyelid—he neither reacts in confusion to being called "baby" nor reciprocates the show of affection, instead simply responding with, "I'm very busy, what's going on?" Busy, eh? So, Mark must be involved in something. Is he working feverishly in the office? Playing sport? Developing a solution to world hunger? No, he's sat in a stationary car, staring into nothingness. While I'll be the first to admit that doing so would be more intellectually stimulating than talking to Lisa, it highlights the disconnect between script and staging. What was so impossible that they couldn't just show Mark in an office, sat at a desk with a pile of papers in front of him and an annoyed look on his face? Or, if that proved too difficult or time consuming, why not just cut the line? It doesn't exactly bring an end to the conversation, so what is its purpose?

Lisa wants to talk about Johnny, but Mark reminds her that he's busy, suggesting they talk about it later. Here, Lisa shows more backbone than she did with her mother. "We'll talk about it now! Whenever you say we'll talk about it later, we never do," she says, hinting that they have an established secret relationship, although this is not confirmed by any of their actions in the film.

After caving in and agreeing to listen to Lisa complain about her mother's desire to control her life and ask him for advice, Mark replies, "Why do you ask me? You've been very happy with Johnny"—despite the fact that Johnny has never been directly mentioned, nor previously alluded to, in the conversation. Is Wiseau worried his audience will lose interest if there's no mention of Johnny for thirty seconds?

"Can I see you tomorrow?" Lisa asks, following Mark's empty spiel. They arrange to meet at noon, and Lisa signs off the call with a mischievous grin on her face.

We then move to an overlong establishing shot of a San Francisco streetcar before returning to the Wiseau residence. Obviously, little time has passed, and we'll have a little more plot development before Mark comes to meet Lisa tomorrow. Oh, no—actually we won't, because here's Lisa, opening the door to Mark. (Why make such a clear indication of the amount of time before they meet if it's not going to feed into the narrative?) Mark enters with a suggestive "Hi, how ya doing?" and the two smile. There is a definite chemistry between them—something that's so lacking between Johnny and Lisa—but it completely fails to fit what the mood should be.

When people discuss *The Room*, Wiseau (rightly) receives a lot of criticism and mockery for his acting, but at least he has the excuse of probably not being of this earth. What are the other actors' excuses? While their performances are occasionally technically acceptable, their complete inability to effectively read even the small amount human emotion present in *The Room* is plain to see. As scripted, the only way this scene works is if Mark acts the innocent, while Lisa works her hardest to turn him to her ways. Mark must be naïve and slightly stupid. Or, Mark must be Denny. Yes, the only way this scene—nay, this film—would work would be if Mark were Denny. Lisa seducing Denny? I'd watch that.

Instead, Mark—who we are led to believe has felt no previous attraction toward Lisa—gazes at her adoringly, while she flirts her hardest. She walks around, stroking him, and Mark never once reacts in a surprised manner. Greg Sestero's performance is that of a man at his first lap dance who doesn't know if he's doing the right thing or not. Look at the way he sits in the chair, with his arms perfectly still on each armrest, like man who is attracted to his host, but terrified of touching her: this is in no way the performance of a man who has innocently gone over to someone else's home and had that person's fiancée suddenly and unexpectedly come on to him. Sestero is terrible in this scene, and I don't just mean terrible by movie standards—I mean terrible by *The Room* standards.

Lisa pours Mark the world's loudest glass of champagne and hands it over, using the classic seduction technique of "stroking the hand slightly too long." "Thank you," says Mark, in wide-eyed surprise, as though he had completely failed to guess she was pouring it for him. Playfully suggesting it's getting hot, Lisa tugs on the ribbon of her shawl and takes it off to reveal *the dress* underneath, while Mark gormlessly eyes her like a forty-year-old virgin. "The candles, the music, the sexy dress. I mean, what's going on here?" he asks. In fact, there are no candles on set, no music anywhere—diegetic, at least—and I'd argue against the sexiness of the dress, but Mark's facial expressions suggest women are a mystery to him, so we give him a break.

Lisa shows Mark just what exactly is "going on" by sitting in his lap and telling him, "I like you very much, lover boy"—Danielle delivering the line as though she has cotton wool in her mouth, combined with the intonation that suggests English isn't even her second language. As she strokes his hair, Mark shrinks back, a big dumb look on his face.

"What are you doing this for?" Mark asks, before it finally clicks, and he pulls her hand away. "Johnny's my BEST friend," he adds, *finally* establishing his relationship within the film's complex cobweb. Lisa pouts like a five-year-old who has been told to go to bed early, insisting Mark forget about Johnny. This is definitely about control now. Lisa is just doing this to show that she can; who Mark is probably doesn't matter. (It's a shame for Denny that he's still probably doing his homework.)

After a few seconds of beard-stroking and soul-searching, Mark decides, "I don't think so," and starts to get up to leave.

"Please don't leave. Please don't leave," Lisa begs him. "I need you. I love you. I dream about you. I need you to make love to me."

It's all a bit much for a first date, but it doesn't seem to put Mark off too much, as he offers only a weak "I don't think so," which is easily reversed by Lisa standing him up and making her move. Which, in turn, leads us to the treat of the film's second sex scene.

This sex scene lasts a slightly more tolerable two minutes and seventeen seconds, as if to suggest Mark lacks Johnny's sexual stamina. Apart from its taking place on the stairwell, and Mark's stubborn refusal to remove his jeans, however, it's pretty much exactly the same scene as that between Lisa and Johnny in the opening chapter—all overdubbed grunts and sappy music. With no difference crafted in the presentation of Lisa's relationships with the two men, the audience feels nothing either way. There's no sense of emotional disconnect between Lisa sleeping with Johnny and Lisa sleeping with Mark—and, therefore, no engendered audience sympathy for Johnny. Without sympathy, the film has no sustainable emotional narrative, and cinema without emotion is not cinema at all. I'm sure Wiseau thought that, in his own way, he was presenting his own searing insight into betrayal, but unfortunately, he seems to have developed his understanding of movies the same way Tony Montana developed his understanding of English—phonetically.

"Why did you do this to me? Why?" Mark whines, clearly having never heard the phrase "It takes two to tango." "We can't do this anymore," he adds. "Johnny's my best friend." The "anymore" indicates that it isn't the first time this has happened. Make up your mind, Tommy!

"You're right. He's your best friend," Lisa replies, seemingly ignoring Mark's desire to cut the affair short and focusing simply on the "best friend" theme that the script will go on to beat to death over the course of the film. She vows that this is their secret, and they agree it won't happen ever again . . . before kissing. It seems the memory issues these characters suffer with stretch beyond saying the same two or three phrases over and over again into doing what they swore they would never do again within thirty seconds of saying so. Of course, the fact that there's another eighty minutes left means we know that this is far from the end of the affair.

In 2013, *The Room* celebrated its tenth anniversary. What are your prevalent feelings about the passing of this milestone?
It's quite a feat, considering my thoughts as the movie played at the premiere, way back when. I was sure that would be the last time anybody saw *The Room.* Let that be a nod to the idea that anything is possible in life. ANYTHING.

Did you ever think you'd see anyone—let alone lots of people—marking the occasion? For example, how did you feel the first time you saw the completed film?
If you would have told me ten years ago that *The Room* would have become a global phenomenon, I would have said you were crazy. But here we are.

Do you ever regret being involved with a notoriously bad film? Did it change your career direction or feelings about acting and/or film at all?
It didn't really change my career direction. I had decided to leave L.A. long before the movie became a hit. But it did take some adjusting. I did study theater and worked as an actor, doing a number of professional plays, and nearly had to join SAG [the Screen Actors Guild] because of the number of union film credits I had. So I wasn't just this kid off the bus who had no acting experience—you know, the classic L.A. story. I actually did have a decent résumé, and had invested a good portion of my life to the craft. Plenty of actors that went on to be huge have been in horrible movies. But in the end, a career in acting wasn't in the cards—which, as you can see from *The Room,* is probably not a bad thing. No complaints on this, by the way. I'm pretty happy with the path my life has taken.

Tell us a little more about your background in acting, and where you were in your life before you got involved in *The Room*.

Earlier on in my life, I got involved in high-school theater, where I first fell in love with acting. Then I went to study theater at Arizona State University, and I quickly moved to Hollywood after I graduated. I remember watching *Pulp Fiction* on the big screen and saying I want to do THAT! Acting really was a huge part of my life back then.

Taking into account the off-the-wall auditions and bizarre director, what made you persevere with the process?

It was the most exhausting audition process I have ever experienced, by far. I mean, Spielberg doesn't hold that many callbacks. But, when a director calls you back, you show up. And you try and bring the best game you can. The story of my audition and first meeting with Tommy Wiseau are the subjects of issue one of *My Big Break* [Haldiman's comic book].[1]

I'm curious as to what you felt about the film and the material while making it. Were people on set at all cynical about the film, or was it more a case of being swept up in the team effort of getting it done?

You'd really never knew what to expect on set. One day you'd be told you're doing the tuxedo scene with no idea as to what that meant; another day you'd start shooting two hours late, because Tommy hadn't arrived yet. A week later, you'd be working with a completely new crew, which probably has a lot to do with the disjointed nature of the photography. In fact, all of this contributed to the end project.

What did you make of Denny as a character, and how did you approach playing him? He's something of a standout character in that his intentions, situation, and background are never quite clear, and as such he is the subject of many theories. For example, I've heard a rumor that Denny was written as autistic, but that you weren't informed . . .

The script has no descriptions of the characters. It is virtually all dialogue. This means we all had to fill in the blanks as actors. Nobody directed me to play Denny as "retarded" or autistic. I always have thought of Denny as a kid who's trying to do his best, but things just never seem to work out as he plans them. I think we've all had days like that. Denny desperately wants to do good by Lisa and Johnny. After all, Johnny has paid for his tuition, which Denny saw as a way out of his orphaned past.

Where do you think *The Room* will stand in another ten years' time?

Good question. I actually interviewed John Waters [cult director of films such as 1972's *Pink Flamingos*] a while back, and he posed me with the same question. Pop culture moves so fast these days. It's so hard to say, but there's something special about *The Room*. Gosh, I couldn't have predicted the last ten years. How could I predict the next ten? That would take all the fun out of it!

Would you act in another Tommy Wiseau project again?
Maybe. On set, he always talked about a vampire movie, which always intrigued me.

What do you think of *The Room* screenings and the audience participation? Do you have any tips for *Room* "virgins," for example?
One of the things that is interesting about *The Room* is that every screening is different. Whether you see it in Seattle, Austin, L.A., Phoenix, or wherever, each one will be different, in terms of crowd participation. The best ones are when the fans are most passionate and not afraid to jump out of their seats and really perform something as a team.

HALF HALF CANADIAN BACON WITH PINEAPPLE

HALF HALF ARTICHOKE WITH PESTO

light on the cheese

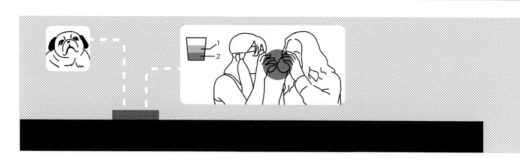

An establishing shot of the San Francisco hills drags us away from the heartbreaking secret of Lisa's betrayal and straight back into Johnny's hectic day-to-day life. After an unnecessarily long shot of him parking in front of a flower shop, we are treated to one of *The Room's* standout non sequiturs: cinema's greatest flower-based sequence since *Little Shop of Horrors.* It's difficult to know where to start. Do we begin with the revelation that Superman was right all along, and that simply adopting eyewear is more than enough to hide your identity—even from a shopkeeper who admires you to the point they feel the need to loudly profess it in front of their other customers? Do we consider how Wiseau possesses so little self-belief that he felt the need to shower his screen id in such praise? Do we simply list surreal quirks of dialogue?

- Johnny's aimed-at-no-one-in-particular "Hai."
- The cheery "That's me," which doesn't actually follow on from the previous line of dialogue.
- The florist saying "Here you go" while grabbing the flowers, rather than when she hands them to him—you know, when you're actually supposed to say it.
- The out-of-the-blue "Hi, doggy!" spoken as though the poor animal has teleported into the scene at that exact moment—and not been sat there all the way through it.

Or do we recognize that all of these quirks—alongside the abundance of other Room tropes such as bad dubbing, awkward extras, and shoddy framing—confirm the flower shop as having been built on the Indian burial ground containing the apex of the Wiseau-verse? It's a microcosm of everything that makes *The Room* what it is.

Meanwhile, back at Johnny's, Lisa is ordering food. Quite why we need to see her do so is anyone's guess. Within a second of her putting the phone down, the doorbell rings—as if the visitor were waiting patiently for Lisa to finish. It's Denny. Considering he barged in unannounced during the film's opening scene, we might wonder why Denny's suddenly decided to start using the doorbell. Maybe he's learned some manners, or maybe there's just ZERO consistency in the way the characters act.

"I'm really busy," Lisa informs him. "Do you want something to drink?" she adds, having apparently absorbed Mark's habit of telling people you're busy but then carrying on the conversation as though it isn't actually a concern. Fans of *Breaking Bad* have long theorized that Walter White, as his alter ego, "Heisenberg," picks up a person's characteristics when he kills them; maybe Lisa inherits people's bad habits whenever she sleeps with them. Can you imagine what would happen if she slept with Denny? What bizarre creature could you create by combining the habits of Johnny, Mark, and Denny? I don't want to talk about it.

Within eight seconds, Denny mentions Johnny. He wants to talk to him. As he says Johnny's name, he looks awkwardly around the room, as if he's checking for surveillance equipment. With the obligatory Johnny reference out the way, we can move on to the second commandment of Every Scene In *The Room*™: someone must mention how beautiful Lisa is. "You look beautiful today. Can I kiss you?" Denny says, raising his eyebrows like Groucho Marx. There is a sweet moment as Lisa looks moved by the compliment—*The Room* in Genuine Human Emotion Shock!—and there does seem to be some real levity as she playfully dismisses Denny's advances. She tells him Johnny will be here any minute, but Denny has to go. Quite why Denny decided to try to call on Johnny when he was obviously so busy is anyone's guess, but the scene ends up doing no more than reinforcing the film's central conceits with hammer-like subtlety: Lisa is Beautiful, and Johnny is the Centre of Life, the Universe, and Everything.

So, what have we learned in the last two minutes of screen time that advances the plot? Literally nothing. Bear in mind, when discounting credits, that this film runs for only ninety-five minutes, yet these two minutes have focused solely on characters buying things. We didn't need to be shown a scene of Johnny buying Lisa's red dress for the opening scene, so why do we need one of him buying flowers? Why must we have another scene of someone looking for Johnny and then telling Lisa she's beautiful? These two scenes in particular stand out as particularly egregious examples of Wiseau's slapdash, thoughtless attitude to storytelling.

Editing is an almost unheralded part of successful filmmaking. For those with a more active interest in not just a film but also the thoughts and intentions behind it, the importance of editing is very clear, although good editing can be an invisible art. The most commonly considered aspect of editing in filmmaking is knowing what to cut out and what to leave in. Martin Scorsese's *The Wolf of Wall Street* was heavily criticized for being too long, its three-hour running time seen as self-absorbed and excessive, but some critics have since come to consider the idea that the editing purposefully represents and reflects the film's self-absorbed, excessive characters and their ideologies. Those characters' abhorrent personalities can be read as so all-consuming as to not only pollute the narrative of the film's reality but also the construction of how the story is presented. By giving us too much, the film subconsciously creates an unease and contempt in the viewer, forcing an extra layer of loathing for the people presented to us without the characters themselves having to do a single thing. This is editing perfected as one of the building blocks of cinema. *The Room* also leaves in far too much, but unfortunately that's because we have a filmmaker with no filter, plus an unerring belief that he could never shoot anything that might be seen as redundant—either that, or he is so convinced of his audience's stupidity and/or lack of attention that he constantly feels the need to spoon-feed viewers key information until it's seared into their minds like some kind of brain tattoo.

Johnny arrives home from work, and Lisa seems genuinely delighted to see him, which is confusing, considering that since their last meeting she's told her mother how much she hates him, and then had sex with his best friend. It's as though Wiseau has edited together two different films—one where Lisa loves Johnny, one where she hates him—in a random order. There's a brief recreation of the opening scene—Johnny gives Lisa something and she reacts—before Lisa asks Johnny if he got his promotion. "Naaah," Johnny grimaces, pulling a face that suggests a recollection of a childhood trauma, and slumps onto the sofa. Lisa pulls her best "concerned" face: a brutal combination of "dyed the hair, but not the eyebrows" at its most comical.

"You didn't get it, did you?" Lisa asks, having seemingly been brought up in a world where saying "no" and looking depressed are ambiguous displays of emotion.

"THAT SON OF A BITCH TOLD ME I WOULD GET IT WITHIN THREE MONTHS," Johnny roars, before relaxing his voice to add, "I saved them bundles." The voice changes, but the facial expression remains the same—as solid as the rock from which it was so haphazardly carved. His continuing complaints of betrayal are interspersed with badly timed cuts to Lisa ignoring him and playing with her flowers instead, as if he is running through football scores rather than discussing a potentially major impediment in his career. Lisa eventually returns the complaints, telling Johnny she has no friends, and that the "computer business is too competitive" (here referencing a career that is never expanded upon or alluded to in any other aspect of the film).

Lisa suggests getting a pizza. Johnny doesn't care.

"I already ordered a pizza," Lisa tells him, oblivious to his disinterest.

"Ah, you think about everything!" Johnny replies, as though it were he who had wanted the pizza in the first place. We don't know why we needed the previous scene of Lisa ordering it to set up this scene, but it's as close to logical causality as the film gets, so we're happy.

Next, Lisa decides that Johnny needs a drink. "I don't drink, you know that!" Johnny laughs. Hard as it might be to believe, given the slurring and general incomprehensibility of his actions, Johnny is straight edge. (Or more likely, he's got his bronze AA chips, and he's desperate to hold on to them.) Lisa looks at him and we hard cut to her walking in from the kitchen, a glass in each hand and a bottle of vodka under her arm. Johnny sits staring into space, waiting for his entrance into frame to awaken him from his cinematic coma. He laughs as Lisa places the glasses onto the table.

Lisa's pizza order has arrived, but it seems that the company in question failed to supply her with the toppings she asked for. What exactly is the timeline for this scene, from Lisa suggesting drinks to the pizza arriving and Lisa getting the drinks? The questions don't stop there. Why do we need a full thirty seconds of Lisa entering the room, pouring vodka into two glasses, mixing it with what looks like whiskey, and then handing Johnny his glass—all in a complete silence that is only broken by Lisa emotionally blackmailing Johnny into drinking it? My head hurts!

After Lisa force-feeds Johnny his drink, we fade to an empty bottle of vodka. By now, Johnny and Lisa are, he says, "tired and wasted." We know they're drunk because, in an act of textbook drunken tomfoolery, Lisa has Johnny's tie wrapped around her head like John Rambo. Johnny is obviously enjoying his liquor, as he gives the kind of satisfied groan he usually reserves for when he's violating a woman's navel and drops his glass to the ground, where it shatters violently.

"You have nice legs, Lisa," Johnny remarks, unprompted, as she laughs uncontrollably.

"You have nice pecs," she replies, still giggling hysterically.

Playing drunk is arguably the hardest thing for any actor to do, and very few achieve it in a manner that isn't cringe-inducing. Nicolas Cage won an Oscar for his portrayal of an alcoholic in *Leaving Las Vegas,* having prepared for the role by recording himself speaking while drunk so as to accurately capture the right cadences.[1] But while that shows it can be done, neither Danielle nor Wiseau is capable of accurately fulfilling the role, and here the scene just feels awkward.

"Come on, make love to me," Lisa demands, her Jekyll-and-Hyde treatment of Johnny roaring on unhindered. Johnny groans and holds his side, obviously in pain—though not in as much pain as the audience, which is about to endure a third sex scene, less than half an hour into the movie. "You owe me one," Lisa insists, pulling him down to the sofa. She rips open his shirt and they kiss awkwardly for a full, horrible ten seconds. There's not even any variety to their kissing style; it's the same movement repeated over and over, as if the cameraman is seeing how long he can wait before someone points out that this is getting creepy. Instead of waiting for the kiss to end, the shot fades into the sex scene, which makes us wonder if, somewhere out there, that kissing is still going on . . .

We settle down for a sex scene that is, in its own way, infinitely more unsettling than the butter-buggery in *Last Tango in Paris.* As the horribly generic R&B music kicks in, Johnny seems to be thrusting into Lisa's abdomen rather than his, ahem, intended target. Perhaps the oddest . . . wait a second, doesn't this all seem strangely familiar? As though you've read it all before? That's because, just like this scene in the movie, it's nothing more than the coverage from the first sex scene, rearranged slightly. What Wiseau saw in the footage that led him to decide it needed to be included again (but with worse music this time) is unclear, but at least it only accounts for sixty-nine seconds of film this time.

After fading to black, we cut to later in the day/week/millennium, where Lisa is sat, clipboard in hand, talking with someone. The strange framing means we can't see who it is.

"So, I'm ordering a party for . . . ," Lisa begins, before pausing awkwardly to remember the name of the man she's marrying. "Johnny's birthday," she continues, remembering. "Can you come?"

"When is it?" is the reply. It's Claudette. Why is she out of shot? It's not as though the reveal changes the context or dramatic trust of the scene. They have a very brief interchange about the party before Claudette unloads her woes upon Lisa. Apparently, her brother Harold wants the house—something that has no relevance to anything in the plot from this point forward—and her hateful ex-husband, Edward, is talking about her. This, too, has no relevance to anything in the plot from this point forward. Finally, she's dying of breast cancer. Again, this has no relevance to anything in the plot from this point forward. This detail is one of *The Room's* most celebrated narrative quirks, and certainly one of its most bizarre, but the way it is tossed aside as some sort of conversation-filler is actually quite offensive. Breast cancer is a life-changing development in anyone's life, yet Claudette's brave admission is greeted with a trite "Don't worry about it" from her daughter, amid a confusing level of irritated eye-rolling between the pair. Quite what Wiseau was thinking during this section is probably beyond the comprehension of any other living creature; it doesn't develop anybody's character or help bring forward the narrative as a whole.

Feeling guilty that they're discussing something that's unrelated to Johnny, Claudette and Lisa soon return to their favorite topic, and once again we get ready to listen to them discuss Johnny in an all-too-familiar manner. This time, however, we get the revelation that Johnny got drunk and hit Lisa. Brushing past the fact that Lisa has seemingly sunk low enough to lie about domestic violence, we're more stunned by the fact that here, after almost nine minutes of events that are little more than ham-fisted reiterations of what has gone before, we've finally landed on something that forwards the plot.

"Johnny doesn't drink!" a shocked Claudette replies, apparently more concerned by Johnny's alcoholism than her daughter suffering from domestic abuse. As Lisa delivers a monologue about how she doesn't love Johnny anymore, the camera cuts to an out-of-place reaction shot of Claudette. Lisa then decides she doesn't want to talk about it—making us wonder why exactly she brought it up in the first place—before adding that she has to get ready to meet a client. Claudette leaves, the sound of the door opening and closing obnoxiously crashing into the mix, and Lisa sits and stares into the distance. Guess that client isn't a very important one.

12

Doggy: A dog, especially a small one.
Dogeee: The correct spelling, according to Tommy Wiseau.[1]

After attempting some of the worst parking of all time, Johnny enters a flower shop, and the scene that follows is a cause of fascination for anyone who comes across it. In researching this book, I asked almost every interviewee what their favorite scene was, and despite the fact that most people said that it varied, the flower shop scene was the most popular recurring answer.

Brock LaBorde offers perhaps the best description of the scene's appeal, which he sums up as being due to its incomprehensibility:

> **It is unlike anything else I've ever seen before. My friends and I had to watch that scene ten times when we first saw it. No matter how many times you see it, your brain just can't process the information correctly. It's like we're all computers who read 1s and 0s, but Tommy gave us something coded in 2s and 3s. It's maddening, but I can't get enough of it.[2]**

A self-serving vignette that wildly crowbars Johnny's popularity into the narrative of the film, the flower shop scene seemingly gets everything backward without even trying to. Basic film conventions are flouted, and the dialogue, timing, and purpose of the scene could not be any more awkward. Even Johnny's progression from the door to the counter is complicated by some spatially confusing editing, not to mention Wiseau's unpredictable walk. Beyond the surface, each viewing rewards us with some new strange detail: Who is that strange lady hanging onto the counter? Why does Johnny carry his flowers out of the store upside down?

And then we have "dogeee." Throughout *The Room*, Johnny begins conversations with the exclamation "Oh hai!" The line appears nine times in the film, but this is the one that has remained the most memorable. The out-of-place, spontaneous greeting to a countertop pooch is not only far removed from cinema as we know it, it also serves no purpose, except perhaps to strengthen Johnny's "good guy" persona. It's probably more accurate to say, however, that it's a reflection of Wiseau's own kind openness. Reports have suggested that Wiseau found the dog on location and spontaneously reacted to it, making this scene perhaps the biggest insight into his own personality. That said, the same story also suggests that Wiseau was confused as to whether the dog was even real.[3]

The flower shop scene was filmed in Wiseau's beloved San Francisco on the very last day of filming on *The Room*.[4] I would suggest that this why the scene so fully encapsulates the tone of the film: hastily shot on location in San Francisco at the end of production, with the idiosyncratic conventions of the auteur now fully bloomed, it captures Johnny/Tommy at his best, excited and enthusiastic, in control of his own destiny and full of the joys of home. Wouldn't you say hi to a dog if you knew that you were just about to complete your masterpiece?

The familiar stock footage, oddly jaunty music, a shot of an empty room waiting for the characters to enter, the exact same overdubbed door sound from the previous scene—it seems *The Room's* getting a little predictable. Just when we think we're getting our heads around the world of Tommy Wiseau, however, he blindsides us with new characters. Who are they? What are they doing here? Now's not the time for exposition; after the bombshell of Lisa's fake claims of domestic abuse, we've surely overdosed on plot advancements, and what we now need is some confusion to help us relax.

The scene that follows is between two friends of Johnny and Lisa, who we will later find out are called Mike and Michelle. They are Wiseau's idea of the perfect couple, their purpose being, theoretically, to heighten the tragedy of Johnny's collapsing love life. I say theoretically because, of course, it doesn't. As this is the first time we have seen the characters, we're more concerned with trying to figure out what is going on rather than paying attention to the dichotomy of the two relationships.

Mike and Michelle gleefully sneak into the Johnny residence like school sweethearts stealing a kiss in the yard.

"How long do we have?" Michelle asks, excitedly.

"A couple of hours, at least," Mike assures her, puffing his chest out in expectation. Their attraction and happiness is eagerly shown to the viewer as they kiss and play with chocolate in a scene that Wiseau surely thought could be straight out of *9½ Weeks* but ends up closer to some kind of *Sesame Street Guide to Lovemaking.*

"Did you . . . know . . . that chocolate . . . is the . . . symbol . . . of love?" Mike says, squeezing the words out as though he's being asked to recite a tongue twister backward, before convincing Michelle to give him fellatio. Before she even starts, Mike—now clearly established as the comic relief—pulls the face of a man chewing on a toffee that's pulling out his teeth.

After being treated to nearly two minutes of characters we don't know badly acting out a scene we don't care about, things get back on track—or at least as much as they ever do in *The Room*. Claudette and Lisa reappear, presumably returning from having a conversation about things that Lisa doesn't want to talk about, and interrupt Mike and Michelle getting dressed. They quickly stand up, Mike with his sweater "hilariously" on backward and inside out.

"Hello? What are these characters doing here?" Claudette asks, voicing the frustration and confusion of everyone watching this scene for the first time. (Claudette as audience surrogate is an intriguing proposition, and it might explain why she spends most of the film annoyed at the stupidity of everything around her.) Lisa explains that they like to come to Johnny's place to do their "homework," before introducing Claudette to Mike, but not Michelle. Does this mean Claudette already knows Michelle? Please, Tommy, give us some idea of the characters' interrelationships! Mike offers a hand, which Claudette rejects with a brutally snobbish air, and the lovebirds exit.

Claudette sits down just in time for Denny to come in and be introduced by Lisa. Surely they'd have met before at some point, though, given how much time they both spend at Johnny's place? Instead of saying hello to Denny, Claudette proceeds to berate Lisa for . . . I'm not sure exactly. Having friends, perhaps? Denny's request for sugar, a cup of flour, and a half-stick of butter also goes down badly with Claudette, who with her acid tongue beats him into a hangdog retreat. Lisa grimaces with displeasure before joining her mother on the sofa.

"Tell me, what does Denny to?" Claudette asks, in a tone that suggests she's asked it before. It seems the introduction of Mike and Michelle into the mix has confused Wiseau as to who knows whom and what they know about each other. I suppose six characters (well, five-and-a-half, since Mike is a 2D caricature at best) *is* a lot to have to remember. The whole thing leads into another touching "Johnny has a heart of gold" moment, with Lisa telling the tragic tale of Johnny financially supporting and wanting to adopt Denny, complete with the usual "listener reacting to a different take" cross-editing.

Suddenly, Mike bursts in to break up the monotony, grabbing frantically for his "book," which turns out to be his boxers, leaving Claudette and Lisa to burst into hysterics. Lisa then doesn't want to talk about it, though what she doesn't want to talk about this time isn't 100 percent clear. This is a textbook example of an inability to craft dialogue that naturally switches from one topic of conversation into another, resulting in pet lines as "I don't want to talk about it" as a way to bridge gaps in the same way one would use "action" or "cut" when directing. Claudette takes this as her cue to leave, and we're treated to a new piano composition—a brief yet foreboding flourish—as Lisa slumps back and painfully says, "Oh my God!" for no reason that we can decipher.

We see Wiseau's confidence as a director growing, now, with the introduction of new characters followed by a new locale—the townhouse rooftop. His failure to get the ingredients he needed from Lisa having killed his cooking plans, Denny has resorted to playing basketball alone as the camera pans across the roof, passing a backless rooftop access point that looks so flimsy that a slight breeze would likely knock it over. We hear the door creak open and a pair of feet menacingly approaches the top of the stairs. Denny turns and stares at the intruder in a rather feeble attempt at evoking the feel of a Mexican standoff. The angle is reversed, and we see Chris-R, looking every bit the WWE reject, slowly walk toward Denny. At this point, the camera zooms in on the door as Chris-R walks diagonally out of shot, shrinking him into the corner and diminishing any sense of size that might previously have been afforded him.

As we cut back to the "Mexican standoff" angle, Denny looks visibly worried. We are then gifted one of the few moments in *The Room* that remotely approaches an attempt at anything "cinematic"—a shakily handled, half-circular pan around Denny that only really serves to highlight how absolutely feeble the green-screen technique being used here is. Denny and Chris-R exchange stock dialogue to bring us up to speed. Apparently, Denny owes Chris-R money, and it'll be there in five minutes. Unfortunately, Chris-R doesn't have five fucking minutes, so he pulls out a handgun, forcing Denny to the ground in a moment of tension that's undermined by the fact that the accompanying dramatic music is so limp that it sounds like it would be better suited to a shot of someone finding a fly in their soup.

Chris-R spends the next thirty seconds shouting, "Where's my fucking money?" ad nauseam; it's as though the actors who were supposed to have interrupted the violence have missed their cue, and he has no idea how to fill the time. This section also includes the film's most amateurish camera angle yet: a close-up of Chris-R's gun that's so off-balance that the gun itself only occupies half of the screen, the other half showing nothing but the blackness of his shirt.

Finally, Mark and Johnny arrive. Despite their having a clear view of the roof from the stairs—plus the uproar of Chris-R's angry yelling—neither seems to have any clue that something is going on until they pass through the doorway. They run over to Chris-R and wrestle him to the ground, with the action shown from the angle of the rooftop access point employed earlier in the scene. Our view is 100 percent clear, offering a clarity that is then shown to have been impossible when the angle switches, and we see Lisa and Claudette in front of the door and

a badly green-screened backdrop. When and how they got up there is a mystery—as is why Claudette is even still in the building, considering she went home at the end of the previous scene.

"What's going on?" Lisa shouts, briefly stealing Claudette's role of echoing the sentiment of those watching at home, as Mark and Johnny unconvincingly grunt their way through hauling Chris-R off the roof and down the narrow staircase. The grunting noises sound worryingly similar to the sex sounds from earlier on. Johnny offers a clearly overdubbed "Let's take him to the police," presumably added in later on, to prevent any viewer confusion over the fact of where exactly they were going to take Chris-R and alleviate any excitement of a potential "Zed's Dead, baby" *Pulp Fiction*–style ending to the film, with Chris-R riding off into the sunset. (That said, wouldn't Tommy make a wonderful Gimp?)

The next ninety seconds are filled with painfully overwrought acting, as Lisa and Claudette interrogate Denny, who admits he owes Chris-R money for drugs. Denny bravely drops the "f-bomb" at Claudette, who grabs at his tasteful yellow-and-purple striped top before Lisa breaks them up and hugs Denny, showing a motherly propensity toward him. For a second, it's almost as though she's a real person, and not just a "manipulative bitch."

At this point, Johnny rushes back on the scene—suggesting it took him a full one hundred seconds to take Chris-R down to the police station, follow full police procedure, give a statement, and then return to the rooftop. Unless, that is, halfway down the stairs, Mark offered to drag the dangerous gun-toting psychopath drug dealer down the police station on his own. Or maybe not, because Mark has silently materialized behind Claudette, placing his hand on her shoulder as he tries to calm her down and maybe lead her off somewhere. Ignoring this, Claudette threatens to call the police, forgetting that the police would already have become involved once Chris-R was taken to the station.

"Why did you do this?" Johnny asks. "You know better, right?" his voice fluctuating to the extent that those nine words contain every tone possible for the human voice box to create (plus a few that it usually can't). Johnny pulls some incredibly pained facial expressions before suggesting, "Let's go home"—presumably forgetting that they're already there.

This episode is genuinely the most irritating of the film's myriad of subplots—a lame "drugs are bad" morality yarn that serves no purpose. Wiseau is obviously obsessed with the American dream, and it seems fair to assume he has taken on board Reagan's War on Drugs as a part of that ideology. This is his commentary on the dangers of drug abuse and, ironically, it comes across as though it was conceived, written, acted, and directed by people out of their minds on PCP.

Incredibly, our next scene is plot-relevant, if repetitive, as it shows Mark on the phone to Lisa. His room is lit by candles, which seems overly romantic, considering he's a bachelor alone at home, but whatever—it's not exactly the most incredulous set decoration decision in the movie. Lisa tells Mark she misses him, that she wants to hear his sexy voice and is thinking of his strong hands holding her body; the camera shuffles almost as awkwardly as we do upon viewing this declaration of love. The scene exists solely to repeat what we already know and remind us that there is actually some dramatic tension behind this seemingly unconnected series of events. To make sure it's absolutely clear to the audience, the pair repeats the exact same dialogue twice—"You just don't care!" says Lisa, to which Mark replies, "I do care!"—in the space of about five seconds.

The scene seems to have sparked Wiseau's memory as to what has happened in the previous thirty-eight minutes, as now Johnny barges onto the roof, angrily chanting, "I did not hit her. It's not true; it's bullshit. I did not hit her." He scrunches his face into an anguished Arnold Schwarzenegger–esque expression. "I did naawwwttt!" he adds, before hurling his water bottle to the ground. We're given no indication as to how Johnny has discovered this revelation, but we're so shocked that a character is reacting to something directly related to a previous plot point that we don't care.

Having vented his anger on the water bottle, Johnny unexpectedly offers a relaxed "Oh hai, Mark!" and walks over to his friend—who, it turns out, has been sitting there the whole time.

"Oh, hey Johnny, what's up?" Mark replies, in a manner so casual that it's clear he somehow failed to notice Johnny burst onto the roof and shout out his frustration at false accusations of domestic abuse. Johnny takes a seat and basks in the glory of a . . . misty, overcast San Francisco evening. Why would Mark be up on the roof in this weather? He claims he's just "sitting up here thinking, you know?" as he plays around with the football he's brought up to the roof with him for some reason, before inexplicably asking Johnny if he thinks girls like to cheat like guys do. (Surely being in the midst of an affair might have answered that for him?)

"What makes you say that?" Johnny replies, wearing an expression of such seriousness and suspicion that, if this were someone who could actually act, you'd guess it to be the first hint of Mark and Lisa's affair being discovered. This is Tommy Wiseau, though, so it's just a coincidence. Johnny adds he doesn't have to worry about such things, as Lisa is loyal to him, making her sound like a foot soldier in a deranged cult.

"You never know," Mark shoots back. "People are very strange these days." Is he trying to plant doubts in his mistress's fiancée's mind?

Johnny listens intently as Mark tells the story of a girl who was sleeping with twelve different men until one of them found out and beat her up so badly that she had to go to the hospital. "What a story, Mark!" Johnny brays, maniacally, at the thought of a young woman being hospitalized as a result of domestic violence. Is he absolutely certain he didn't hit Lisa? He sure seems to get off on the idea of violence against women.

Attempting to move our sympathy back to the betrayal facing Johnny and away from the hospitalized woman, Wiseau crams in the most awkwardly placed line of expositional dialogue in cinema history. "I'm so happy I have you as my best friend," Johnny says, "and I love Lisa so much." Just in case the previous fifty times this information has been bestowed upon us hasn't stuck. This prompts a discussion about the merits and demerits of women.

The Room is very odd in that it's predominantly a film about the love a man has for a woman, but underneath that it's worryingly misogynistic. While it portrays its female characters variously as hateful, manipulative, conniving, and overly dependent on men for financial security, sexuality seems to be the main concern. Throughout the film, Lisa is constantly defined by her sexuality. Not once does a male character praise her for her intelligence, charisma, or abilities; it's always "Lisa's beautiful," or some focus on her skills in the bedroom.

Attempts to reconcile women as real people as well as sexual beings are often badly handled in mainstream cinema due to it being a traditionally male-dominated industry. Whether it's the treatment of the "damsel in distress" or just a female character's inability to deal with situations as efficiently as men, women are all too often given the short end of the cinematic stick. But it doesn't have to be this way. James Cameron, for example, has repeatedly proven himself to be a Hollywood filmmaker who can consistently craft strong yet feminine female characters. The most famous is his take on the Ripley character in *Aliens,* but Sarah Connor in *The Terminator* is another good example. She initially seems to be defined by an archetypal female role—the mother—but we slowly come to see that she is more than capable of looking after herself. Kyle Reese, the masculine soldier from the future, fails to kill the robot antagonist, but Sarah—possessing strength and determination that would, more stereotypically, be associated with a male—is able to do it. She becomes the hero without sacrificing her femininity.

So, how does *The Room* address the subject of women? Well, Mark tells us he broke up with a woman because she was bad in bed, to which Johnny replies that Lisa is "great, when I can get it," thereby showing about as much respect for his fiancée as he would a sex toy. Mark complains about how he just can't understand woman, criticizing them for being too smart, too stupid, and just plain evil. Johnny sees this as justification enough to declare him an expert on the subject and pushes for more information on his private issues. Mark—seemingly not ready to confess just yet—storms away moodily, as Johnny steals the football away from him, for no other reason than that it's needed for the next scene.

CHRIS-R
DAN JANJIGIAN

INTERVIEW

You got involved with *The Room* through your roommate originally playing Mark.¹ Can you tell me about that?

He was the original guy! We were in Santa Monica at the time, and I had actually just moved out to L.A. I told him I wanted to get involved with some different acting. I'd taken lessons, and I just wanted to get started with the training. He told me there was an independent movie that he was doing [that] was looking for a guy that was built like me and I should check it out. That's how I got introduced to Tommy Wiseau and *The Room*.

I think yours was quite a typical audition for *The Room* in that it took place in a parking lot . . .

Yeah, it's funny, [Tommy] was sitting in a director's chair, and I came out, and my roommate had warned me, "He wants to know or at least feel like you know something about acting." He gave me a couple of key phrases that would make me sound like I was knowledgeable in acting. I remember he told me to talk about the fact that there's two methods of acting, Stanislavski and Meisner—"Tell him that you like Stanislavski"—and so I basically just went in and bullshitted my way into the movie.

Your scene was reshot on the rooftop set but was originally shot in the alleyway, and the original version can now be seen on the DVD special features. What made you go back?

When he originally shot it, it was aggravating, because we were there for weeks. I didn't know if I had multiple scenes or what the deal was. We weren't allowed to see the script, but then we kept shooting the same scene every day. There would be days when we'd be sitting there all day, waiting to do something, and nothing would happen. Imagine sitting there for weeks, and you're in a movie where there's only one shot of you that was probably, all told, about a minute, a minute and a half long. It was very odd, because you kept expecting there to be something else—your character to be reintroduced—but since we had never seen the entire script, that was the only scene that this guy was gonna have. When I left, I had to come back. I think I was at the grocery store, and Greg Sestero said, "Come back in, Tommy wants to reshoot the scene," and I'm like, "Dude, I'm not going through that again." I basically negotiated it out, and I said if I'm coming back I'm getting paid, because I don't have another two weeks to spend. They agreed, and I came back.

The Disaster Artist paints you to be one of the few people to stand up to Tommy and negotiate your own terms.[2] Why was that?
The reason I wanted to do the movie to begin with was to learn and to get reel—something that I could use for other auditions. I had been told it's not about the pay, and it's really about getting film of yourself. At that point, I had a good relationship with Greg. I knew I could get the film I had shot down at the alley. He had promised me copies of that. I honestly didn't care, because nobody expected that film to do anything.

In the behind-the-scenes footage of the rooftop scene, there's a really funny moment: Tommy's directing you and explaining about a gun falling off the roof, and you look very confused. What was it like to hear some of the things that he came out with?
It was frustrating. You'd just laugh about it with everyone else on the shoot. Everybody was going through it, and the directions that we were given were just so ludicrous. For example, I told him over and over again [that] I couldn't imagine this guy just continuing to say, "Give me my fucking money, give me my fucking money." There was nothing else to be said, and I told Tommy, "Even if I'm yelling, let me at least yell something different." But that's all he wanted, over and over again—because that is *so powerful*! It was so inane that it just got to the point that it was funny. We just kind of went with it. If someone's telling you the same thing over and over again and everybody else is doing it, you're like, "All right, whatever, it's your movie. It's my job to do what you want me to do, so fine, I'll do it."

In terms of building a character, do you have any theories about who Chris-R is or what his backstory is?
That was the funny thing. Since we couldn't read the script, we had to base everything on what we were told. My first scene—I thought it was gonna be one of many—my one and only scene was this guy who was coming up to a drug dealer. I tried to invent some kind of backstory about what this guy did: how would I feel if someone borrowed money from me? You try to take yourself to a place, but then you take it to a new level—you try to get a loan back from a friend who apparently bought

drugs from people. Who knows how long ago? You're trying to take yourself to a point where you get really hammed up about that. You've got nothing to draw from; you have to really make it up. You have to really make up some wild shit. You have to create some kind of character. In *Entertainment Weekly,* they called it a plot cul-de-sac, because it went nowhere.[3] I don't pretend for a second that there was anything special about my role.

Have you developed any further theories on Chris-R since? Like, what the R stands for? Why the hyphen in his name? What drugs he was selling?
People would ask me, and I joke and say that the *R* stands for "Ridiculous." I have no idea. Every time we do a Q&A, I make up something different, like Denny was on Viagra because he was so fired up on trying to get Lisa. Every time we do a one-on-one, it's just kind of funny to come up with different ideas of what it could possibly have stood for.

That neatly leads on to asking you about the screenings and the cult that has grown around *The Room.* What were your first experiences? Did you know about it straight away?
The guy that played Mike [Scott Holmes], he called me up and he was like, "Hey man, they're doing another showing in L.A." I was still living in L.A. at the time, and the movie was very, very new. I didn't really wanna go and see it again—I'd seen the premiere. He was like, "Dude you've gotta come, people are coming to watch the thing, they're dressing up as the characters," so I went down there, and I was shocked. There were so many people there, and after the film was over, we kind of came in late, and there were people grabbing us and wanting to talk, and I was like, "What's going on?"

One guy I talked to said he'd seen it close to a dozen times. I couldn't even believe it had played a dozen times at that point. It probably had only been out a couple of weeks, if that. My timeline might be wrong, but it didn't feel like it had been out more than a short amount of time. It was crazy. I went to a couple in L.A., and then, when they were bigger, in New York, Seattle, Chicago, Boston, Texas . . . I've been to several of them, obviously. I remember the one in New York—that was the one that blew me away. It was a theater that held close to 1,000 people. There was a big balcony area. They had mugs with our faces on them, like coffee mugs—they were super cool, my kids think they're the coolest thing ever. They had the bobble-heads up there; they actually had a band that had instruments in the theater, and I dressed up as Chris-R. That was probably one of the most fun times I've had. They did an awesome job of putting it together.

You were saying that your kids were excited about seeing you on a coffee mug. What did your family and everyone else think about _The Room_ when they first saw it?

Actually, I'll tell you something funny: my brother and sister went to a showing in New York last night, and I had no clue. My parents told me that they went. I was like, "You're kidding!" My brother is one of the main guys at Bellevue Hospital—he is a GP—and [he and] a huge group of people went to see it in New York last night. My parents have never seen it, obviously my kids have never seen it—they want to rent it, and I was like, "No, don't rent it, you will be so bored out of your mind." I had to warn them—I said, "Look, I'm swearing," and they were, like, "No, we know, its OK." It's one of those things. They love it. They think it's the funniest thing ever.

This has been going on for over ten years now and keeps getting bigger, and there are people all across the world that love _The Room_. Do you think it will just keep growing and growing?

My honest answer is I can't believe you're talking to me about this right now—it boggles my mind that it's playing. The fact that you are in England and know anything about this movie is mind-blowing to me. Greg has sent me a picture of one of the billboards of a theater in London, with a bunch of people lined up around the corner. I was like, "You've got to be kidding me, how did that grow there?"

The rooftop is not a good place for Denny to go. After his previous altercation with Chris-R, our young hero reaches the heights, only to be angrily bumped into by Mark, who doesn't even raise his head to offer an apology as he departs. "He's cranky today, ha ha ha," Johnny explains. Denny double-checks the pair's plan to see a movie together, asking what they intend to see. Johnny considers this question for a brief moment before replying, sagely, "Don't plan too much, it may not come out right." This, it seems, is a man who lives a life of such awesome spontaneity that even checking whether there's something you want to see at the local multiplex is to risk killing life's thrills. Given the hashed-together nature of *The Room's* script, it's quite easy to see Wiseau as someone who would espouse the positives of not even thinking about the next line of a screenplay ahead of time. We can clearly see that this is his mantra for filmmaking.

The all-important question of what movie they will see is left hanging temptingly in the air as Denny suggests that they "toss the ball around." Treating the ball as some kind of "talking pillow"—with neither character speaking without holding it in his hands—leads to some unnatural pauses, and the ball even appears to get lost on the way at times. Denny uses this "father-son" moment to drop the bombshell that he's in love with Lisa. You see! That weird, repeated flirting *was* going somewhere, after all! So, Denny, tell us: what is it you love about her? OK, she looks great in a red dress . . . what else? That's it? No reference to her shining personality, her intense intellect, or anything else that might suggest he has confused her with a real human being? No, Denny admits that he's just confused, which is a logical state for anyone who's admitting to feeling any emotion other than contempt for Lisa.

Johnny tells Denny not to worry—love is OK—as a strained version of the main theme echoes in the background, sounding as though it were recorded in a wind chamber. It's at this point that Wiseau's unique message to the world—his raison d'être—finally echoes forth from Johnny's mouth. "If a lot of people love each other, the world would be a better place to live." Tommy Wiseau essentially made *The Room* to inflict his life philosophy on the world, and it turns out it's so trite that the only place it should really be released is on a *My Little Pony* greeting card.

Johnny goes on to tell Denny that he trusts him and Lisa, thereby revealing that half of the scene's true motive is to reinforce sympathy for our unwitting protagonist. Denny, out of nowhere, thanks Johnny for paying his tuition fees, thereby revealing the other half of the scene's true motive: to remind us that Johnny is the BEST guy EVER, and that all who mistreat him are inherently evil. Johnny then asks Denny about Betty, whom Denny says he loves and plans to marry and have kids with after he graduates. You'd have thought that such an important person in Denny's life would at least have been alluded to before, but this is the first and last we hear of the mythical Betty. In fact, given the slim likelihood of someone actually wanting to marry Denny, she probably is mythical. Still, it seems he's moved on from Lisa pretty quickly. Maybe Johnny's greeting-card speech had more going for it then we give him credit for.

Johnny leads Denny away to get some food, with the scene pointlessly made ten seconds longer than it needs to be by showing the pair walk across the roof toward the rooftop access. If you had a set as mind-blowing as The Roof of Johnny's Townhouse, though, you'd want to show it off as much as you could.

One of *The Room's* best-known idiosyncrasies is the fact that while two cameras were used during filming, they weren't employed separately, and they used different formats. Confused by the differences between 35 mm and HD, Wiseau paid for a custom-built Frankenstein's Monster dual-camera rack, resulting in every scene being shot twice, from two slightly different angles, creating some interesting continuity issues.[1] We've already seen several instances of problems caused by cross-cutting shots of actors who are obviously reacting to an alternate take, but the following scene, featuring Lisa and Michelle, takes this to a whole new level, and contains some of the most egregious continuity errors imaginable. To try to detail them all individually would take an eternity, so for now, just keep an eye on Lisa's wine glass, or the hand Michelle is using to prop up her head as she sprawls on the couch. Not that anyone need these pointers—the errors are so bad that we don't feel a secret sense of superiority at spotting them but rather a secret sense of shame at watching a film made by people who were so indifferent to the results that they couldn't be bothered to correct them.

"So, how's Johnny?" Michelle asks. The camera holds its position as Lisa explains that he didn't get his promotion.

"Is he disappointed?" Michelle asks, before we cut to an angle from over her shoulder, showing Lisa magically holding the wine glass that was previously set on the table.

"Quite a bit," Lisa replies. "He got drunk last night." We cut back to the view of Michelle and see Lisa taking the wine glass that had previously been in her hand from the table and silently mouthing, "and . . ." before cutting back to the angle over Michelle's shoulder. Sighing deeply, Lisa decides to try speaking again, this time successfully adding, ". . . and he hit me." This indicates that everything from Claudette's breast-cancer revelation until now all took place on the same day—which, of course, isn't possible. Lisa needs to get her story straight if she wants to convince people that Saint Johnny is slap-happy, as she's currently accusing the teetotaler of getting drunk and hitting her on consecutive nights. Or maybe the script has no concept of its own narrative timeline.

"He hit you?" a startled Michelle replies. "Are you OK?"

"Well, I don't want to marry him anymore," Lisa deadpans.

"What?" Michelle asks, with a look on her face that makes it seem like Lisa is considering ending the relationship because Johnny farts in bed rather than because he hits her.

"Johnny's . . . OK," Lisa purrs, apparently dropping the domestic-abuse angle, "but I found somebody else." She describes her illicit lover as "his best friend," adding, "He lives in this building." Unsurprisingly, Michelle guesses that Lisa is alluding to Mark, before insisting she tell Johnny before somebody gets hurt. Lisa says she doesn't want to hurt him, once again upending a line of inconsistent character motivation that swings—sometimes in mid-sentence—between her hating Johnny and merely feeling her love fade away.

"Well, if you care so much for him, why cheat on him?" Michelle asks, posing a question of such insight and logic that it must have been an ad-lib. Lisa insists she loves Mark and tells Michelle not to guilt-trip her about it, before Michelle chillingly predicts that something awful is going to happen—conveniently ignoring the fact that something awful has been happening for forty-four minutes and twenty seconds already.

We cut to a brief five-second shot of Johnny walking toward the front of his apartment building and casually picking up a newspaper that has been left in front of it. (Doesn't he have a mailbox?) This feels so similar to Bela Lugosi leaving his house in *Plan 9 from Outer Space* that there's almost certainly a case to be put forward for Wiseau having been possessed by Ed Wood. We then cut back to the exact same point where we left the Michelle/Lisa conversation, as though they had simply frozen for a moment while the world focused on its true epicenter. This time, however, we're viewing things from a ridiculous top-down angle, which is retained for the next section.

"Your secret's safe with me," Michelle promises, as we overhear the door opening and Johnny entering. He stands still as the girls make a toast to infidelity, before stepping toward them.

"Hello Michelle," he says. "I heard you. What secret?"

Lisa insists that it's between them, and Michelle says, "Hi, Johnny." Johnny completely ignores her and instead asks Lisa if she's bought a new dress. Sensing the tension, Michelle gets up to leave. The previously docile Johnny seems irked by Michelle as he point-blank refuses to move his legs, which are propped up on the coffee table, until she asks him to. There's a brief medium shot of Johnny—because we haven't had a shot of that for almost three minutes, and Wiseau knows what the punters want—before we cut to Michelle at the door. As she exits, Michelle turns to her and says, "Remember what I told you," in an almost Denny-level misreading of the situation. She might as well have said, "Lisa, stop having an affair!" before leaving.

Left alone with Lisa, Johnny presses her to reveal her secret, before matter-of-factly stating, "I never hit you." Lisa doesn't seem particularly surprised that he knows what she's been saying about him, so we're supposed to simply accept that Johnny somehow found out; Wiseau has evidently decided that this wasn't important enough to get its own scene, even though the Chris-R/Denny confrontation needed three minutes of running time. Lisa looks decidedly guilty, and with his calm yet depressed delivery, Wiseau is surprisingly effective at eliciting our empathy. Yes, I'm praising Wiseau's acting, but don't worry, there's little to praise hereafter.

After that, the bizarre stage directions require Johnny to get up, remove his jacket, and throw it next to Lisa, telling her that she should have no secrets from her future husband.

"You sure about that?" Lisa asks. "Women change their mind all the time," she adds, talking just the way that women do in real life.

"You must be kidding, aren't you?" Johnny guffaws, cleverly offering a line where the delivery is as bad as the grammar.

"Look, I don't want to talk about it!" Lisa replies, angrily. "I'm going to go upstairs, wash up, and go to bed," she adds, seemingly forgetting that it's only dinnertime, so going to bed now seems a very contrived way to get out of discussing their issues. Johnny explodes into a rage, shoving her down, yelling, "How dare you talk to me like that!"—showing signs of actually becoming the abusive monster Lisa has accused him of being.

Quite how Wiseau thinks he can portray his character as someone who would angrily place his hands on a woman and yet still maintain our sympathy is one thing, but the fact that he follows this up with Johnny almost breaking down in tears and begging Lisa to talk with him is the definition of pathetic, serving only to reinforce why Lisa wants to get away from him. This tragic example of an emasculated man-child is intended to be romantic, as Johnny continues to swing between violence and desperation. "I could not live without you, Lisa!" he bawls, as a justifiably terrified Lisa tries to leave. "You're lying, I never hit you!" he adds, suddenly, with an air of relative calm completely at odds with the frantic hopelessness previously displayed, before switching back and grimly hollering, "You are tearing me apart, Lisa!" butchering the James Dean reference in a way that's so memorable that the line is now sadly more closely associated with *The Room* than it is with *Rebel Without a Cause.* Lisa yells at him, understandably questioning his hysterical nature. Once again, Johnny "lovingly" shoves her down, but this time Lisa gets up and leaves to go upstairs, stopping only to say, "Don't worry about it, everything will be all right," for absolutely no reason at all.

"Don't worry about it," Johnny says comfortingly. "I still love you, Lisa." The pair then trades goodnights. At dinnertime. In broad daylight.

After such nerve-shredding tension, we need some comic relief, and it dutifully arrives in the next scene, as Mike catches up with Johnny, who is walking aimlessly around an alley near their apartment for no other reason than that the script needed him to be outside for the purposes of this scene. Mike regales Johnny with a blow-by-blow account of Claudette and Lisa walking in on him and Michelle earlier on. Tommy, if it wasn't funny the first time, it certainly won't be funny the second time—even with Mike's best bug-eyed expression. Mike does, however, justify the scene's existence by ending with the immortal line, "She's showing everybody . . . me underwears" (with "everybody" here referring to all of two people).

"That's life," Johnny replies, at a loss as to why Mike has told him this pointless story, and unsure of how to react to it. Luckily, his quandary is disrupted by Denny, who shows up, fortuitously, football in hand. Denny tries to convince Mike to join them in a game, but Mike is resistant, saying he has to go meet Michelle and "make out" with her. (What man in his late-twenties would feel the need to announce to everyone that he was going to kiss his girlfriend?) Johnny and Denny eventually press-gang Mike into competing, and they break out into a ball-tossing competition so casually framed and acted that Mike isn't even on the screen for half of it. The whole thing feels like a backstage excerpt taken from a DVD extra. You could call it cinéma vérité, but it's not. It's just bad.

It seems the alley is the new cool place to hang out, as Mark appears from nowhere to join in the male-bonding session. Denny reveals the "me underwears" story to Mark, even though he wasn't involved in the original conversation, so shouldn't know about it. "Underwear? What's that?" Mark asks. Given that he keeps his jeans on during sex, I guess it's understandable that he doesn't know enough about how clothes work to be aware of what underwear is. As Mike protests, the camera switches focus and inexplicably centers on the wall between him and Mark, leaving both of them half out of shot on the edge of the screen. Mark pushes Mike for more details and then lightly forces the football into him, though the camerawork and editing make it pretty difficult to tell what is happening. Ignoring the relative lightness of contact, Mike sells it like a fleet-footed soccer player in the opposition penalty box and goes down violently, crashing headfirst into some conveniently placed rubbish bins. As the others pull him to his feet, Mike assures them he's fine—while looking blankly into the distance, as if reacting to a brick to the head rather than a simple tumble. Johnny offers his traditional over-the-top "great guy" promise to assist Mike in any way possible. Mark helps Mike home, and Johnny and Denny also exit, leaving us to wonder, once again, what the hell that was all about.

16

MICHELLE
ROBYN PARIS

INTERVIEW

You came to *The Room* via an ad in *Backstage West*. I wondered if you could describe your memory of seeing that ad, and the process that followed?

Sometime in early 2002, I saw the ad and sent my headshot in for the role of Michelle. I had basically forgotten about it, until I got a call about a week later from Greg Sestero, asking if I could come to the set for an audition. I was in a play in Hollywood that night so I offered to come early. When I showed up to the Birns & Sawyer[1] parking lot around 3:30 p.m., I was the only actress there. I met Greg, who introduced me to Tommy, who asked me questions about my background—why I wanted to be an actor, what roles I had played in the past, etc. We talked for maybe ten or fifteen minutes before the other actors arrived for the audition. Tommy said, "I like you. I think I give you de part, but I don't know. You have too many freckles. We have to airbrush dem out" [with makeup]. He told me that he got his freckles airbrushed out every day. Incidentally, the make-up artists reported that the worst day on set was the day they had to airbrush Tommy's ass.

After the other actors arrived, I was paired with Greg Ellery to read the "chocolate is the symbol of love" scene while Tommy's DP filmed it. After we read scenes, Tommy put the actors in front of the camera and barked orders like, "You just won the lottery! Go!" and, literally five seconds later, "Your best friend just died. Go!" If the person didn't cry on the spot about the best friend, Tommy would say, "Your best friend died and you're not even crying. What kind of friend are you?" The entire audition took place in the parking lot. A total of about forty actors auditioned that day, including all of the actors who ended up as extras in the party scene at the end of the movie.

A week went by, and then I received a call from Greg Sestero, who invited me to a callback. Again, the audition interfered with my play, so I asked if I could come later, and he agreed to see me around 10 p.m.

on the movie set. When I showed up, another actress was there as well. Tommy had narrowed the role of Michelle down to the two of us. Tommy asked us questions about eating chocolate but didn't want us to read any dialogue or do any acting. I remember exchanging wide-eyed concerned looks, like, *what the hell are we doing here?* But we both stayed and auditioned for the part. That's the life of the struggling actor—you audition for everything, never knowing where or when your break will come.

One day, I got a call from Greg Sestero out of the blue, around 3 p.m., asking how fast I could get to the set. So I jumped in the car and headed over to the Birns & Sawyer parking lot. When I arrived, someone handed me a few pages of the script, and literally within twenty minutes I was filming the "chocolate is the symbol of love" scene wearing the same outfit I wore to the set. This was standard operating procedure for Tommy. I went from not knowing if I'd booked the part of Michelle to literally filming a scene from the movie within a ninety-minute timeframe.

You came to *The Room* late. Were any alarm bells ringing as a result of being hired as a replacement?

When I auditioned for Michelle, I was told that the previous actress playing Michelle [Juliette Danielle] had switched roles and would now be playing Lisa. I understood that the actress originally playing Lisa had been let go due to "creative differences." While this could have sounded an alarm, it seemed somewhat reasonable. I had no idea how many of the actors had quit or been fired—like, five or six—and that the shoot had already been going on for months!

Only after I got the part of Michelle and started spending time on set did I hear the horror stories from the cast about the quitting, firings, and other shenanigans that characterized the lunacy of the making of *The Room.* A few days into my time on set, I learned that Tommy had already shot half the movie with other actors playing various roles, and he was reshooting everything from scratch with the new actors. Yeah, at that point, alarm bells were blaring, but I'm not one to back out of a commitment. I had agreed to play Michelle, and we'd already shot a few scenes, so I stuck with it.

I've always wondered if the hiring and firings left any noticeable awkwardness or bad feeling among the cast/crew, or if it was par for the course, as it were . . .

I didn't notice any bad blood on set. There was a sense of camaraderie among the cast and crew—the type of bonding that can only be accomplished by going through battle together. As a group, we were perplexed and mystified that this movie was getting made, and that somehow Tommy had the money to make it and the balls to write, direct, produce, and star in it when he seemed to have limited talent and experience.

Tommy blew through three crews, each of which quit when he refused to pay them in a timely manner. When a new crew was hired, they'd arrive with a positive attitude ready to work. A few hours or a day answering to Tommy would kill any enthusiasm they once had for the project. It became a big joke for everyone who was on set. Everyone was in on the joke—except for Tommy.

What was your first impression of Tommy and the production when you arrived?
Before I moved to Los Angeles, I heard stories of all the crazy people who lived here. Growing up in the southeast [in North Carolina], Los Angeles is characterized as this faraway fantasyland where nobody who is normal actually lives. So, when one of my first auditions in Los Angeles was with Tommy Wiseau, I just figured that, yeah, here is one of those L.A. esoteric wackos I've heard about. He wore a black wifebeater, sported long, dyed jet-black hair, clearly got regular chemical peels and tried to pass himself off as twenty-five years younger than he actually was. I normalized Tommy in my mind because I thought he blended in with the mythology of weird Los Angeles. Turns out, he is about as crazy as L.A. gets. Oh, the naiveté.

Is it fair to say that Tommy was almost the only person on set not in on the joke even at that point?
Definitely. Tommy took *The Room* very seriously. He perceived it as a great American drama, on a par with *Citizen Kane, A Streetcar Named Desire,* or *Rebel Without a Cause.* He fashioned himself as the next James Dean, but he was more of a rebel without a clue. On the *Room* PR materials, he advertised fake reviews from fictional journals, touting himself as the next Tennessee Williams. It was much later, after he realized that audiences were crying tears of laughter, not sorrow, that he changed the *Room* marketing materials and started calling it a "quirky new comedy."

Your delivery of some of the more . . . let's say "idiosyncratic" dialogue is well handled, and you somehow make lines like, "Tricky, Tricky!" and the "XYZ" part seem natural. Did you have to work hard with the script?
Thank you! No, I didn't get much time to work on the script. Tommy gave me my scene pages usually a day before—or sometimes minutes before—we were to shoot something. I asked Tommy for a full copy of the script, but he refused to let any of the actors read *The Room* script because he said he thought we would steal it. The result was that I never knew where my scenes fit into the context of the film.

Before shooting a scene, the actors typically met with Sandy [Schklair], the script supervisor, and together, we'd heavily edit the dialogue. What you see on screen is probably about half of what was actually written on the page. Some of the dialogue was completely unsayable, and there were even more non sequiturs and tangential monologues than what you see in the movie. So, we'd have maybe an hour to work on the edited scene before shooting it. I did my best to sound natural—it wasn't easy!

How do you see Michelle as a character?

Michelle alternates between being Lisa's supportive sidekick, giggling conspiratorially when offered juicy gossip, and serving as the Greek chorus, expressing random moral outrage and concern over Lisa's shocking betrayal of Johnny. Since I had no idea where any of my scenes fell in the context of the entire film, I basically asked Tommy what he was looking for in each scene and did what he suggested. I naively trusted—at least at first—that he had some kind of plan for Michelle's character arc—which was, of course, a preposterous assumption.

***The Room* does not portray women well. I wondered if you had any feelings about the tone and themes of the film?**

I find the film so ridiculous and its characters so one-dimensional and clichéd that it's hard to have a serious discussion about the themes and tone. The women are blatantly cartoonish and immaturely crafted; as a result, I can't find them offensive, because I can't take them seriously. The fact that the crowd laughs uproariously at the sexist clichés reinforces how ridiculous we all think they are. It's like being offended at something a four-year-old says. Who cares? It's from the mind of Tommy Wiseau.

There's a scene in the movie where Lisa and Michelle randomly start beating each other with pillows. I remember Juliette and I met ten minutes before shooting that scene. After a few takes, Tommy said, "I don't believe you are best frieeends. Do what best friends do, okaaaay? Girls hit each ovver wit pillows." Sure, that's what I do with my best girlfriends, over a nice glass of wine. I think the issue is that Tommy doesn't understand the way real people operate. "Do you understand life? Do you?" Tommy doesn't.

The men in *The Room* don't fare any better than the women. It's basically: We are men. We play football. We wrestle with our bros and pick fights at the drop of a hat. We have affairs. We are so weak, we think with our dicks and we can't say no to a "sexy woman." Yeah, the clichés about men in *The Room* are almost as bad.

How do you feel about the movie now, and are you surprised it's still around?

I'm not surprised it's still around at all. Seeing *The Room* in the theater is this frenzy of laughter, fun, and witty banter. There a zealous, comical, frantic energy that's so communal, and I've never seen it replicated anywhere else.

I told my husband back in 2002 when we were shooting *The Room* that I thought it was so bizarre and funny that if anyone ever saw the movie, it might get a cult following. There's just something about Tommy. He's hilarious, he's compelling; he's a one-of-a-kind character. You can't take your eyes off him. I had such a hard time keeping a straight face on the set, particularly during the party scene at the end of the movie. The fighting between Tommy and Greg was just so staged—I was repressing my laughter so much, I had tears streaming down my face. It was like trying not to laugh in church. I was convinced on that day, if anyone else saw *The Room,* if it somehow saw the light of day—people would love it.

How many times have you seen the film now, and what has been your experience of screenings?
I love going to *Room* screenings. I've seen the movie about seven or eight times, the last time being this past April 5, 2014, at the Regent Theatre in Westwood near UCLA. Before that, I saw the movie at the Sunset Laemmle in Hollywood in 2012, and Michael Cera was in line behind me. I spoke to him, and he said he was a big fan of *The Room,* which was really cool. He offered me some great advice when he suggested that I completely embrace the cult craziness.

YOU KNOW WHAT
THEY SAY
LOVE IS
BLIND

Claudette and Lisa return to Johnny's apartment to find the door unlocked. Rather than checking whether someone is in the house, though, Lisa expresses concern at her mother's tiredness. Which is interesting, considering she showed absolutely zero concern at her mother being diagnosed with cancer, but we all have different priorities in our lives. Could this tiredness be a result of the cancer? Of course not, as cause and effect are alien concepts in the Wiseauverse. No, Claudette is actually tired because she's been up all night worrying. Is it the impending breakdown of her daughter's engagement causing her to lose sleep? Again, no: Claudette is worried about her friend Shirley Hamilton, who wants money to buy a house. She reveals that she asked Johnny to help with the down payment, but he declined, calling it "an awkward situation," which Claudette felt was selfish. Err . . . excuse me? In what world does someone ask their son-in-law to lend money to their friend—presumably someone the son-in-law doesn't even know—and then denounce them as being selfish when they say they can't? Sadly, Claudette has devolved from being a relatively interesting character who sticks up for Johnny to another in the long line of people who unreasonably criticize him. Lisa insists that she doesn't love Johnny and then bluntly announces that she "had sex with someone else," using a tone of voice that surely no one has ever used to speak about sex to a parent.

It's at this point we have a four-second cutaway to Johnny peering from behind the stairwell, displaying a powerful look of . . . vague indifference to the revelation that his fiancée is cheating on him. He was *in the room* all the time! Why Wiseau chose to keep us in the dark about Johnny being at home instead of making us aware of his overhearing of the conversation is questionable. The tension of watching as Lisa unwittingly reveals her lies to Johnny would have been palpable—for *The Room,* at least—and might have added some much-needed actual drama to this "drama." Instead, he went for the brief hand-on-mouth surprise, which only lasts one viewing, and dramatically neutered the scene before it even had a chance to grow into the centerpiece of the film that it should have been. All this while ignoring the fact that Johnny's place is so small that he'd have been impossible to miss anyway.

This is not an issue solely with *The Room,* but one that has increasingly become a trend in movies, especially in the horror genre. The aim of the horror movie is to provide that memorable scare—the one we'll tell our friends about, and that will then convince them that they need to hand over the money for the movie ticket. However, a genuinely tense, foreboding, *scary* atmosphere is hard to create, and doing so takes time. As pop culture marches toward increasing disposability, few mainstream films are seemingly willing to take the effort to attempt this endeavor, lest it fail to reap the financial rewards at the box office. As a result, found-footage movies currently reign supreme, offering the perfect mix of cheap budgets and high profit margins. However, movies like *Paranormal Activity* aren't *frightening* but simply *surprising;* they rely on one-off shocks to spark a reaction, instead of the perfectly built-up mix of atmosphere and pacing that a film such as *The Exorcist* provides. As a result, once you know when the "bang" is coming, there is nothing left to frighten you, and nothing to re-watch; the result is ninety minutes spent waiting for fifteen seconds' worth of one-shot scares. That's not cinema, that's a carnival trick, and it's why such films prove worthless once they are finished (if they even manage to feel worthwhile during the first watch). Tension is an art and a challenge, but it's a challenge that pays off; it's why the end of *The Godfather,* where we see the heads of the other four families killed while Michael's child is baptized, is still involving on a fourth or fifth viewing. The absence of this tension is why the dramatic elements of *The Room* are so lacking that Wiseau eventually had to rebrand the film as a black comedy.

"Who is it?" asks Claudette of the identity of her daughter's mystery man. Lisa, surprisingly, doesn't want to talk about it. "Why would you bring it up in the first place?" Claudette asks—not unreasonably—before we yell that it's because the narrative doesn't require Johnny to know the identity yet, and Wiseau couldn't find a vaguely interesting or plausible way for this to happen. Couldn't Johnny have found a used condom on the floor, or something? Anything is more believable than hiding in fairly plain view on the stairs.

"If you think I'm tired today, just WAIT until you see me tomorrow!" Claudette scolds, pointing a finger at Lisa as though telling someone you're going to be tired is the biggest threat imaginable. Then, relying on their telepathic link rather than any audible dialogue for our benefit,

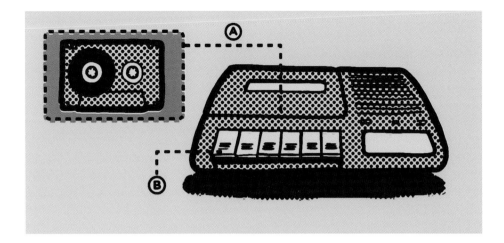

they both leave, without ever giving any indication as to what they came to the apartment for in the first place. Would it have been too much just to have Lisa pick up a pair of car keys or something, to at least make their thirty-second visit offer more than just the delivery of plot spoilers to Johnny?

Ignoring the fact that he clearly has enough evidence to confront her with already, Johnny decides he must undertake a devious scheme to entrap Lisa in her web of lies. Deciding that the phone is the most effective method of doing so, we watch for almost a minute as Johnny awkwardly fumbles around in his attempts to connect a cassette recorder to the back of it. There isn't time for the script to answer where Johnny found this magic device, which records sound forever and automatically stops and starts upon the receiver being picked up, but the early 2000s were a magical time, so different from our own. Why he considers this the best way to catch her out is not made clear, but after completing his task, he gives an inappropriately suspicious smile; it's as though he's glad that he's being cheated on, because it gives him a chance to do some spy work. With that, he stumbles up the stairway, clinging to the central pillar as though he's on a ship in a vicious storm, holding on for dear life.

So, who can Johnny talk to about his problems? We've only been introduced to Mark so far, but surely a man of Johnny's wit and repartee must be swimming in friends and associates? This question is answered typically awkwardly, as there's a cut from Johnny's trudge upstairs straight to a new character, who we see sitting down playing with his fingernails. Johnny pours them both a drink—which we assume is water, since the script made such a fuss of Johnny's abstinence earlier on—and handily introduces the new character to the viewer by saying, "I don't understand women, Peter." This, and the later reveal that he's a psychologist, is pretty much it for character development, but we needn't worry, as in terms of the story, his contribution is negligible. What we can figure out for ourselves, however, is that Peter specializes in a very particular area of psychology best described as "oversimplified, clichéd statements taken randomly from agony-aunt columns."

The action starts with a medium shot of the two sat down in Johnny's living room—which is so dimly lit that it looks like a different set, despite the fact the scene is taking place during the day—before cutting to a close-up of Johnny that was obviously shot at a completely different time, as the lighting is totally different, and his posture has completely changed. His eyes shifting nervously, as though he's reading cue cards, Johnny reveals his worries. "I have a serious problem with Lisa." Halfway through his confession, he gulps an "um" that sounds so out of place, and so different in pitch, our ears tell us it must have been dubbed in from a separate take. "I don't think she's faithful to me. In fact, I know she isn't," he continues, as Peter tries his hardest to look like he cares. Wiseau stumbles awkwardly through the rest of the story, clearly struggling to remember lines that aren't focused on offering to help someone at any time, or saying "Hi," and he completely vaporizes any emotional context for the scene—a confusion only heightened by the inconsistent editing switching back and forth between takes of Johnny in which he's clearly not looking at where Peter is actually sat or stood.

Peter eventually suggests that Johnny should confront Lisa. "I can't confront her," Johnny replies. "I want to give her a second chance." If you don't want to confront her, we wonder, why have you gone to the trouble of concocting that ridiculous DIY wiretap? Is the plan to simply find out who the secret partner is, accept that the love of your life is knocking off someone on the side, marry her, and get on with it?

As Peter continues to offer the kind of advice you'd more closely associate with a man who can't actually spell psychology rather than one who undertakes it as a profession, the doorbell rings. Johnny gets up to answer the door, and the camera swings out of the way to let him by, resulting in the camera holding on Peter's now-empty chair for an awkward second or two before cutting to Johnny answering the door. It's Mark.

After exchanging greetings with Johnny, Mark shouts out "Hey, Peter," which is completely ignored by the snooty psychologist.

"We're just talking about women," Johnny slurs, making us reconsider whether it is just water he's been drinking.

Mark looks on guiltily, the heavy handed sad-piano soundtrack reminding us that it's Mark who's causing all this distress for poor old Johnny. There's a lot of potential for some interesting narrative and character development here, as for the first time Mark is faced with the fact that Johnny may be aware that something is going on, and he somehow has to find out just how much he knows. How does he do this? By admitting to a fake affair and then trying to change the subject, of course.

Mark claims he's seeing a "very attractive" married woman who, for some reason, Johnny wants to meet. When Mark says no, Johnny asks, "You mean she's too old or you think I would take her away from you?" Peter and Mark laugh, though it's unclear whether they are laughing at the "joke" or Johnny's delusion that any woman in any situation would possibly plump for him over Mark and his model looks. Mark's entry into the conversation, meanwhile, seems to have had a powerful effect on Johnny and Peter's short-term memories. Peter asks Johnny to tell them about his problems, despite the fact he's already heard all of them, causing Johnny to angrily reply, "Peter, you're always playing psychologist with us"—despite having asked Peter to play psychologist with him not two minutes earlier.

Dumping an extra character into the mix seems to have caused Wiseau to completely forget what is going on, as Mark's reaction to hearing more about Lisa and Johnny's problems is to announce that he's making decent money and is thinking about moving to a bigger place. While we consider whether somebody has managed to cut out two pages of the script by accident, Peter replies, "Look you should tell her the truth: you're doing it for your girl, right?" which does not seem to be connected to anything either Mark or Johnny have actually said. Johnny pushes the non sequiturs further, saying, "Uh, you're right Peter. Is she getting a divorce, Mark?"

Quite how Johnny has linked Mark buying a bigger house to him hiding something from his mistress is quite puzzling, but Mark brushes it off. "You guys are too much!" he says. What? How has the conversation gotten so derailed within three sentences? It does make us wonder about the mind-set of the filmmakers that such a confusing mishmash of sentences could possibly make it into the final edit. Surely someone must have known that the conversation was senseless. Was Wiseau—the world's least suitable candidate to expound on auteur theory—simply so in control that he ignored the view of everyone around him, or had everyone else already reached the point of not caring?

Relieved that they've moved on from discussing Lisa's extra-curricular sex life, Mark continues to steer the conversation off into irrelevancy. Finally managing to shoehorn in a reference to San Francisco that isn't stock footage, Mark asks if the others are planning to run Bay to Breakers, the city's annual footrace.

"Sure," says Johnny, whose mouth continues to move silently.

"Nah, I'm not doing it this year," says Peter, with his back to the camera.

Peter's refusal to take part in the marathon prompts Johnny to launch into arguably his most embarrassing character quirk. (Yes, he has a habit actually more embarrassing than his navel fetish.) Calling Peter a "little chicken," Johnny breaks out into a cheeping sound that seems to coincide with the exact moment his voice decides to break, especially the last drawn out "cheeeeuuurrrreeeurrppureeee," which may actually be the most ridiculous noise ever captured in the history of recorded sound.

All hyped up on the memories of Bay to Breakers, Johnny bumbles on unintelligibly as we lose 50 percent of our brain cells in protest at an already largely irrelevant and overlong scene plumbing the depths of how witless and mundane it can become. This somehow crashes into the "interesting" story of how Johnny and Lisa met, which simply boils down to him meeting her while working at a coffee shop during his penniless first few months in San Francisco.

"What's the interesting point?" Mark asks, understandably.

"On our first date, she paid for dinner."

I guess you had to be there. In *(500) Days of Summer,* the heartbroken Joseph Gordon Levitt is told, "Henry Miller said the best way to get over a woman is to turn her into literature." Wiseau—having botched a novel and a stage version of *The Room*—decided to take revenge upon his particular demon via the medium of film. Nowhere is this more apparent than here, in the scene that most closely rides the waving line between Wiseau himself and his screen persona, Johnny, and that contains nothing that couldn't have been condensed into about a third of its six-minute running time.

Within seconds of Johnny winding up the conversation by asking the others if they want something to eat and going into the kitchen, the door opens, and in step Lisa and Denny. After a few perfunctory greetings are shared, Mark gets up to leave, and Denny steps over to a nearby curtain to gaze through the window. The tone of the conversation is really strange, as if it's taken from another movie. The camera switches between extreme close-ups of the secret lovers' faces; Lisa flirts and Mark tries to brush it off with protestations that he's got to work early, the music swelling grandly behind them. There's a brief cut to Denny, who looks away from the window, shooting Mark a suspicious glance. A subplot of Denny's gradual

suspicion would have been interesting but, unfortunately, this is taken nowhere, so, to all intents and purposes, Denny's expression could simply be because he's noticed it's started to rain and he's left the washing out. With the tension of being in something vaguely watchable proving too much, Mark leaves abruptly, with Peter following behind, neither of them feeling the need to tell Johnny why they've suddenly skipped out on the dinner plans (or to close the door behind them).

Ignoring the fact that there are now three empty seats in the room, Denny and Lisa sit on the floor. Denny pushes Lisa about the wedding, saying Johnny doesn't seem very excited about it, even though it's only a month away. The idea of the affair taking place with the wedding so close could actually be kind of interesting, but it's not taken advantage of. Lisa insists she's happy and tells Denny she needs to talk with Johnny. They then walk offscreen, with Denny proving to be the one friend the couple has who is polite enough to remember to close the door.

As one door closes, another opens, and we're back on the roof, this time with Peter and Mark. Now, it's fully understandable why Mark is there, toking away on a joint, but why has Peter decided to take a trip up top? Have his psychology qualifications bestowed him with actual mind-reading capabilities? We're treated to the traditional "person walking from door to other person without talking before sitting down" shot, before Peter says, "It's a good place to think up here, isn't it?"

Mark sarcastically asks if Peter intends to put him on the clock before offering Peter some of his stash. "You want some?" he asks. "Its good, bro"—the uncharacteristic bro apparently added because that's how people who take drugs talk, man. The fact that Mark is smoking weed here seems somewhat incongruous, given that it plays no further role in any part of the story, and doesn't really define his character in any way. A personal theory would be that Wiseau—who has already shown a fairly strong anti-drugs stance in the Chris-R sequence—misguidedly thought that associating Mark with an illegal act would further condemn him to his audience.

Unfortunately, Mark seems to be smoking the sort of weed that, rather than making you high and placid, makes you immediately depressed and prone to violent bursts of rage. After Peter tells him he looks depressed, Mark replies, "I did something awful. I don't think I can forgive myself." This actually adds a weight of meaning to his abrupt exit earlier on, and finally gives us an action by a character with some motivation—which is actually shared with us! Mark approaches the roof edge, fatalistically adding, "I just feel like running . . . or killing myself—something crazy like that."

The green-screened city skyline coincidentally turns into a purple haze as Peter once again tries to convince Mark to stop smoking, before casually asking, "You're having an affair with Lisa, aren't you?" This also adds weight to why Peter has followed Mark to the roof, giving Wiseau two-for-two in terms of characters' otherwise unreasonable actions being explained with later details. If only he hadn't failed to do this in the other 1,000 examples of strange behavior thus far!

Enraged by this accusation, the drug-addled Mark decides that the only logical reaction is to try to throw Peter off the roof. The two scuffle like women in their eighties before Peter pushes Mark away.

"Sorry," Mark says, which seems like quite the understatement.

"I'm fine," Peter replies, brushing off the attempted murder. Given how irritating and smug Peter is, I doubt this is the first time someone has tried to kill him, so it's probably water off a duck's back. The interaction is further complicated by the fact that the film never really conveys any close relationship between Mark and Peter; they seem like acquaintances who occasionally cross paths through Johnny, rather than being part of a larger set of friends. Peter's quick forgiveness and eagerness to resolve the issue of Mark's role in Lisa's infidelity don't ring true; this would have been a more emotional and successful scene if Peter had not been introduced just five minutes earlier, as some stop-gap between Johnny finding out about the affair and then discovering who was actually involved.

Kicking over the roof-top patio set, Mark is the subject of a close-up as he paces around, angrily confessing the truth but placing all the blame on Lisa. What a gentleman! Peter offers advice so lame the camera doesn't even bother cutting to him, so we're left with Sestero's over-the-top "reaction faces" until we cut back to a wide shot.

"Don't sleep with [Lisa] again," Peter concludes, before delivering a scathingly harsh character assassination of her, calling her a sociopath (suggesting he doesn't actually know what the word means). I bet his parents were so proud when he got that psychology degree, but he must have found it in a bin. We have one last chance for some horribly shaky green screen as the camera pans across from a close-up profile shot of Peter over to Mark.

"Whatever, Peter," Mark says, dismissing the advice, and the two leave.

18

The casting process of *The Room* seems to have been one that was utterly unique. What was your experience of that?
While the casting process was different from normal film casting, it wasn't that different from someone mashing up a stage casting process and a film casting process. So, it was different, but not extremely different. Also, I hadn't been auditioning for years at that time, thus my frame of reference was much smaller.

A scene in *The Disaster Artist* shows you challenging Tommy early in the filming.[1] The incident seems to be one of a number of recorded incidents in which attempts to help Tommy were met with stubbornness and/or suspicion. Was this a pretty typical incident?
I did mention that it would be best for Greg to have a contract when he took over the role, as I was just trying to help out with the project. I came to find out this was a normal reaction from Tommy on set, which I attributed to the fact he was dealing with so much at the time, he didn't want other complications brought up or he felt he needed to be in control of the situation. After that, any suggestions or ideas that occurred to me, I brought up to Greg or whomever was responsible in that area on set.

Further to the last question, can you describe Tommy as a director, and what it was like to work with him?
Tommy has a unique vision when working on a project. Sometimes that is conveyed successfully, sometimes it isn't. He certainly doesn't have the horror stories of some of the other directors in Hollywood. I think, at his core, he does try to take care of the people in his projects, but his frustration isn't expressed in the best manner at times.

It seems to me that Peter is the butt of a lot of the jokes, and despite being an intellectual professional, he is presented as somewhat pathetic. I can't help but feel there is an element of masculine grandstanding there, as though to reinforce a point, and I wondered if you had any thoughts on Peter's role in the group and as a character.

I see Peter as the voice of reason, the everyman; a touchstone of normalcy in the story of betrayal and violence that is *The Room*. He tries to help his friends, but they are destroyed by their own choices. This does make him the straight man when it comes to a lot of the humor in the movie, but whether it's pathetic or just enduring the chaotic nature of life is something for each viewer to decide.

The Bay to Breakers scene with Johnny, Mark, and Peter is one of the most bizarre in cinema history, and is pretty hard for an audience to follow. How did you approach even trying to comprehend the script?

Peter is essentially the Cassandra—i.e. *The Iliad*—of the movie. He predicts things that are going to happen, yet everyone ignores his warnings. Thus, I approached the character as one that cared for all his friends, did what he could to help, and was longsuffering in their mistakes afterward. When it came to the nonsensical story aspects, I just performed the scenes as best I could with those motivations in mind, knowing it was Tommy's movie and I'd give him the scenes as he wanted them.

Peter infamously disappears midway through the movie, owing to your own time constraints and the film overrunning. Did this leave any bad feeling?

I felt bad having to leave the project without completing it. I never want to put someone in a position like that, as it could potentially kill the project for everyone involved. But I communicated the conflict prior to filming starting and reminded Tommy of it with what I thought was enough lead time to shoot the rest of my scenes before I had to leave. I feel I was as professional as I could have been in the situation. Whether that leaves some bad feelings with any of the others, you'll have to ask them.

How do you feel about the character of Steven? Do you wish you'd been able to finish the film yourself?

There really isn't much explained about Steven. Greg did what he could with what little he had. I thought all those lines would be best if given to Denny, since he had so little to do in the party scenes. Of course, I wish I could have finished the shoot. I don't like leaving a job incomplete. However, not having to figure out how to deliver that "atomic bomb" line was a nice reprieve.

How do you feel about the movie now, and are you surprised it's still around?

The movie is what it is. I've done a number of indie projects and they've all had differing levels of success. I'm surprised at any movie that is still playing for fans in theaters after a year, much less after eleven years.

How many times have you seen the film now, and what has been your experience of screenings?

I don't keep count of how many times I've seen *The Room*. If I had to guess, it is probably around a half-dozen times. I enjoyed going to *Rocky Horror* screenings when I was younger, so screenings of *The Room* have been fairly fun for me. It was at the first of these fan screenings that I had my first celebrity ask for a picture and autograph for *The Room*. Bobcat Goldthwait will always have that dubious distinction.

How has *The Room* affected your life over the past eleven years?

I learned quite a bit about what to do and what not to do in making a movie on the set of *The Room*. I also met a number of people during and since then that have been friends and co-creators on other projects. The notoriety of working on *The Room* has gotten me opportunities in my career, which is always one of the hurdles in acting. Plus, fans recognizing me and coming up to say "hi" always brightens my day.

Lastly, I've heard you commend Tommy for making the film and achieving a final product. What do you feel the legacy of the movie will be?

To be honest, the legacy of the movie isn't in the story of the film itself, but instead the making of the movie. Greg's book, *The Disaster Artist,* proves that the story of someone struggling against all odds while chasing their dreams is a story that resonates with a large group of people. If anything, I hope it encourages more people to chase their dreams in spite of the odds against them, and eventually succeed by reaching their goal, not necessarily just becoming famous for doing something. Creating is the hardest thing to do, so completing a creation needs to be recognized as a success in and of itself more often.

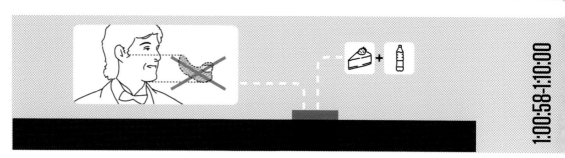

The metaphorical cat that is Lisa's cheating is now well and truly out of the bag. The fact that Johnny doesn't seem to consider overhearing Lisa's confession as suitable evidence to confront her means that the wedding is still going ahead. This scene starts with Johnny on the phone, awkwardly shifting from side to side, as if he's trying to simulate an earthquake. There seems no other reason to open on this action than Wiseau's desire to show off his ability to realistically act out a telephone conversation. Unsurprisingly, it's pretty bad.

Perfectly in time with the end of the phone call, a door opens offscreen. Before the camera even has time to swing around to capture the mystery entrant, Johnny spoils the surprise with an "Oh hai, Denny," before saying something else that has been removed from the sound mix, leaving an awkward silence as Johnny's jaw flaps about like a goldfish adjusting its false teeth. Finally regaining the gift of speech, he adds, "Nice tux! You look great." Denny has his ball in hand, meaning some bonding is going to go down at some point soon, though you have to wonder why anyone would bring a football to a wedding photo shoot. It's Denny, though, so a logical action would actually be an illogical one by his standards—it's like the bizarro world.

Next, the doorbell rings and Peter enters, closing the door behind him. Before the five seconds required for him to sit down have elapsed, the doorbell rings again. It's nice to know Johnny's friends are so punctual—arriving conveniently within ten seconds of each other—but why Peter didn't know there was someone following so close behind him, or why the person in question didn't get Peter's attention to tell him that he was so close behind, is lost to the ages. Fortunately, we can soon stop worrying about it, as in walks Mark—CLEAN SHAVEN! Now, I personally don't consider that worthy of caps lock, but the film certainly does, as it zooms in tight on Mark's face, and a melodic harp strum echoes magically to herald the arrival of the Adonis.

Johnny seems particularly enthralled by Mark's new look. Unfortunately, his reaction comes at precisely the moment his Xanax kicks in, blubbering, "You look great, you look—ub—bub—baby-face, uuhh." Denny spontaneously suggests a game of football, as though it's the most natural thing in the world for the four men to do at this point. Peter, in an uncharacteristic moment of clarity, says no, and the others mock him with the least enthusiastic "cheep-cheeps" ever, with the three actors really struggling to hide their embarrassment at partaking in the ritual. The increasingly depressed Johnny in particular looks uninterested in participating in the mockery, bending his legs to look like he has rickets and then lifting his arms up and down as though carrying the world's lightest dumbbells. The whole thing is so disturbing that the film mercifully cuts before they have time to finish, saving them further embarrassment.

Apparently, though, like calling Marty McFly "yellow," this taunting is enough to make Peter agree to anything, and the Fantastic Four soon find themselves outside. As they toss long throws to each other, Denny shrilly calls out the others' names like a five-year-old excited at finally being allowed to play with the adults. Mark throws an unnecessarily long pass that Peter races after obediently. With Mike unavailable to take the pratfall, Peter tosses himself to the ground like an Olympic diver, landing right in front of the camera. Despite his arms being spread wide as we cut, he comfortably lands on his hands, facing in a completely different direction to that which he had been falling, as though he twisted his entire body around in the split second between the shifting from the medium- to the low-angle shot. Perfect tens all round.

"Gee, Peter. You're clumsy," says Denny, squeezing the words out through gritted teeth and displaying a look of annoyance rather than the amusement that was intended. Peter then tells the others he's done. They help him up, and we're treated to a *Reservoir Dogs*–style shot of four pairs of shoes marching past the camera. The whole scene took thirty-six seconds. We will never get that time back.

After some pointless exterior shots, the obnoxious hiss of a coffee machine establishes that we're in a new location: the local coffee shop. Over the top of a coffee machine in action, we hear an order for a "slice of cheesecake and a bottle of water." Remember that—it's important. The camera cuts to a side view of the counter, and we see a couple ordering a large peanut butter cup with extra whipped cream, a cheesecake, and a coffee. I've given you the full detail of these characters' orders because the movie considers them vital enough to include them in the scene, so they must be important, right? Not an inch of film wasted. Anyway, having established that this is a functional, successful coffee shop—for those of you worried about the post-9/11 economic circumstances facing San Francisco—we move onto Johnny and . . . oh, no we don't; we get to watch two more extras make an order. Why? Oh, well . . . let's see what they're ordering at least. The man orders a bagel and a . . . something. Exactly what he orders is not entirely clear, as he's drowned out by the background noise of the previous couple scraping their chairs back to sit down. The woman orders a slice of cheesecake and a bottle of wat . . . Wait. This is oddly familiar. Yes, they've actually used a sound bite of the order over the earlier establishing shot of the coffee machine. Not only was the earlier use of the clip completely unnecessary, but Wiseau didn't even have the imagination to come up with a fifth original order—and that's taking into account that he's already used "cheesecake" twice. This is the beauty of *The Room*— it even messes up scenes of people ordering coffee.

Finally, our heroes arrive, with Johnny—pillar of the local community—greeting the owner with a warm "Oh hai, Susan" and ordering a medium hot chocolate. Mark orders a "medium, also" mint tea. They take their seats, and we see the previous customer sitting behind Johnny, clearly drinking something even though he had not yet been served his drink when shot from the previous angle.

"I'm so tired of girls' games," Mark whines. The exchange ends with Johnny staring out the window and offering the most depressed "You should be happy, Mark" he can muster. Their drinks finally arrive, with the waitress semi-aggressively trying to convince them to order cheesecake; it seems like they still have some left, despite every other customer having ordered it.

Mark asks Johnny about work, and Johnny's dead, emotionless eyes stare grimly through Mark's soul as he recounts the good news that the bank has a new client who will make them "bundles." Mark presses him, but Johnny admonishes him for his rudeness in asking for something confidential, before changing the topic: "Anyway, how's your sex life?" This would make a lot more sense if Johnny knew that it was Mark who Lisa was cheating on him with, but he doesn't, so the opportunity for Johnny's behavior to make sense once again disappears like tears in rain. Mark blows the question off as the waitress brings them the bill. They've been sat down for forty-nine seconds—yes, I counted—but this acts as a wake-up call for Mark that he has to go. Why would you meet someone for a coffee when you *literally* have less than a minute of free time? The two trade ridiculous fist-bumps as they set up a meeting for 6:30 at Golden Gate Park. "Okey dokey, brah," says Johnny, as he walks off. Mark fixes a deep and meaningful stare into the distance as we close the scene.

Presumably you've noticed by now that each of these chapters is focused on roughly ten minutes of the movie. At the moment, we're less than four minutes into this section of our odyssey, but the next six

Football Attire Johnny

cut-out doll

minutes give us almost nothing to discuss, as the film descends into an absolute content vacuum. There's a three-minute sex scene, just shy of ninety seconds of Mark and Johnny frolicking in Golden Gate Park, and a minute of footage that reaffirms the rarely covered fact that Mark and Lisa are having an affair. Although there are certainly parts of the film that are much stupider, the complete irrelevance of this section is frightening. Nothing better highlights the inadequacy of the editing of *The Room* than these three superfluous scenes. It's actually quite frightening to think of the great films that have been shackled into a slim-lined form because they had too many ideas to fit into an acceptable running time. There's a scene in *Hakuchi,* Akira Kurosawa's adaptation of Dostoyevsky's *The Idiot,* in which Setsuko Hara's character enters the living room and takes just two steps before a hard cut warps her across the room and brings her back just in time to see her at the table at the opposite end. Apparently, the original edit included the full walk across the floor, but Kurosawa's distributors were so concerned about the film's five-hour-plus running time that they brutally and mindlessly edited the film until it became, arguably, the director's worst work. Upon being told that the studio wanted to cut the negative in half, Kurosawa angrily suggested they had better cut it lengthwise.[1] Upon hearing his film wasn't actually feature length, one imagines Wiseau suggesting, "Let's have more sex scene and film the exercising at park, huuh?"

Although Mark's face at the end of the previous scene made it appear as though he was having reservations about his philandering, within thirty seconds he's involved in another sex scene; it seems his "anxious" face is actually his "horny" face. Anyway, Lisa leads Mark into the bedroom, her hands around his waist.

"What's going on here?" Mark asks, displaying, in his inability to read social situations, a naivety bordering on ignorance. "I like you very much, Mark," Lisa explains. "Come on, Johnny's my best friend," Mark weakly insists. Do we really need this dialogue? If you haven't yet realized that Lisa wants Mark and Mark is Johnny's best friend, you certainly wouldn't have had the attention span to watch the previous one hour and five minutes of *The Room.* We then launch into another sex scene—because hey, sex sells. To give Mark his due, he does seem to have more of an idea than Johnny does, though his stubborn refusal to take off his jeans does make us wonder whether this is actually sex or just heavy petting. Another thing is that Mark seems to be doing significantly more appreciative grunting than Lisa. Considering she is the one doing all the chasing, she doesn't seem to be getting much out of the sex. Other than that, there's nothing to see here. Move along.

After collectively zoning out for two and a half minutes that feel more like two and a half hours, we come back to reality with the familiar "jaunty piano over San Francisco" establishing shots, which leads into a kind of montage of Johnny and Mark playing around together. There is some dialogue, but it's almost all perfunctory, and drowned out by the unreasonably loud music. They toss the ball around a bit before Johnny playfully wrestles Mark to the ground and . . . that's it. It adds nothing, it means nothing, it is nothing. If the previously alluded-to editing of *The Wolf of Wall Street* makes the characters seem as though they're leading bombastic, self-important lives, the editing of *The Room* makes its characters seem as though they're living fruitless, meaningless, and ultimately worthless lives. How very Zen.

It's been fifty seconds since our last establishing shot of San Francisco, so another one is squeezed in before we return to the living room of Johnny's apartment. Lisa is sweeping up when the doorbell rings. "Who is it?" she yells. It's Mark, who "comically" announces himself as "delivery man." Lisa scrunches up her face in a way that suggests she either doesn't get the joke or she actually thinks it really is a delivery man and doesn't remember having ordered anything. Eventually, Mark comes in, with the camera pointlessly panning across to show his entrance, only to pan back with him as he walks across the room to stand beside Lisa.

Unable to combine the skills of talking and walking, Mark waits until he's completed his unexpected journey before breaking the silence. "Wow, so you . . . err . . . going to be ready?" he asks, to which Lisa replies, "How do you mean that? I'm always ready. For you." Mark tells her he means for Johnny's birthday party, helpfully reminding us that the film *did* have a plot at one point, which prompts Lisa to change into her "party dress." Unfortunately, this means Lisa nudity—something that Wiseau obviously felt hadn't been covered enough already.

"What are you doing?" the permanently dumbfounded Mark asks, as we prepare for yet another sex scene—only to see it cut short by a crashing knock on the door. The audience exhales collectively, as we come to the frightening realization that in no point in history have people been so relieved that sex hasn't happened.

20

MLADEN MILICEVIC AND
CLINT JUN GAMBOA
INTERVIEWS

Interview: Mladen Milicevic, Composer of *The Room* Score

Mladen Milicevic's unusual score for *The Room* has become one of its most recognizable idiosyncrasies, and is, to some, the composer's best-known work. As such, it might come as a surprise to them to hear that Milicevic holds an MA in experimental music composition, has won several music prizes for his compositions, and is professor of recording arts at Loyola Marymount University, Los Angeles.

Take me back to the beginning: how did you become involved with *The Room?*
Through the editor of *The Room,* Eric Chase. We worked on a project before that, which was called *Reality Check.* I was told to watch *A Streetcar Named Desire,* it's a theater play, music was totally inconsequential, but anyways I watched the movie. Then I met with Tommy and watched *The Room* with him.

Was the movie complete at that point?
Pretty much, yeah. It was done; they were just doing the sound post-production, but the picture was cut. It was all done. Tommy was paying cash, and to me, the movie was bizarre in a way that I kind of—in a perverted way—wanted to enjoy it. I did the first theme—you can find it on YouTube[1]—the original theme, which they didn't like because it was too dark. I did it as a tragedy, because the movie is a tragedy, but they wanted something lighter. Then I came up with the *Room* theme, which they loved. I think in the end, the way the whole thing turned out to be, I think what they picked worked better.

I guess originally he asked you for something dramatic, and you delivered that. How did Tommy respond when you first did it?
Well, you see, it wasn't Tommy—it was Eric. Tommy did not participate in the score. The only thing that he was interested in was all the rights that

I sign off work for hire, and I signed them all off—it doesn't matter. Eric just made comments in the beginning about the main theme, and once I changed that, I had no major interaction with either Tommy or Eric, so I just finished it, I scored it the way it is, and that was it.

What guidance did you get from Eric?
Well nothing, you know. They said, "Oh, this is too dark, give us something totally light," but then I came up with that—the theme—kind of joking.

Did you intend any comedic value, or were you scoring it straight?
Scoring it straight, as if this was going to be a regular movie. That was it, so I finished, and Tommy wanted to have a CD out. I gave him all the rights because I didn't care—actually, even if I didn't, the only way composers can make money out of a movie is if it airs on TV. He wanted to have a CD, so then he just took the file straight out [of the movie] and printed it straight onto CD, and he asked what should be the titles [of the tracks] and I said, "Whatever you want, who cares?" What was funny is that there was this band who made the songs—I didn't make the songs, I just did the score—but the songs for the love scenes, that was the band that he found. So if you listen to the CD, because it wasn't mastered, you have pretty much background score music at the level that it was in the movie—just soft, soft, soft—and then a song comes in and just blasts through your ears. [The CD] was released in the days when records still existed. You had *The Room* next to John Williams and all the others.

Can I ask you about the style of the music? It's quite unique. What kind of instrumentation did you use?
It's all synthesizers; it's all samples. I played everything, no live instruments, no nothing—I just played all the stuff and put it together. So yeah, that's how it was done—I score low-budget movies and documentaries that cannot afford real musicians. It's all one-man-band show. That's how *The Room* was done.

When did you first see the final product?
There was a screening, the opening night in June, or July . . . it was broad daylight, and he had the searchlight in front of the theater. [Tommy] came in a white limo with his poster on it; they were giving welcome packages with little printed material in there, which is the pictures from the movie, lines such as "Where is the money?" and stuff like that. The CD was in there, so that was like a little gift for the audience. The screening started, it was one of those Laemmle theaters—those artsy kinds of theaters—so the screening started, and probably like twenty minutes into it people started giggling and laughing and some of them

left. After that there was a party that was great—an upscale restaurant that was pouring expensive wine and stuff like that—and that was it.

A couple of years after that, I think the movie was playing somewhere, and of course, Tommy put this big billboard in Hollywood that was there for like eight years or something. I can claim that my name was in Hollywood on a billboard longer than Steven Spielberg's. The movie played, and I said to a friend of mine who was a DOP, I said, "You gotta go see this." So he went there, sent me pictures that he took in the theater during the screening, and he called me from there and said, "What's going on? How could you do this? You have no idea what was going on." I didn't know what was going on, so I went to see it, and it was what it was, you know, a big performance, and then just it took off and everybody . . . younger kids started going to the movie for screenings. They learned all the lines, you couldn't hear anything because they were making comments, playing football, throwing roses, plastic spoons, and all the stuff that they do.

Do you get asked a lot about *The Room?*
Well, I do. It's kind of strange. One of the funniest things was I went to Wesleyan University, for the eightieth birthday of my professor, Alvin Lucier, whom I came to the United States with, who was like a big-time avant-garde composer. I got my masters at the Wesleyan University, which is where John Cage published all his books. So, Alvin was celebrating his birthday, and of course they were playing all his compositions and all the students came. When the undergrads found out that I scored *The Room,* they went crazy. It's so bizarre that even in my home country of Croatia they have a *Room* fan club. I have a cousin in Amsterdam who Xeroxed the tickets his sixteen-year-old daughter bought, and she was practicing for the screening, learning all the lines and looking forward to the week ahead.

As a serious academic and someone who does this for fun, what's your lasting feeling about being involved with *The Room?* Is it a happy experience?
Well, it was definitely a great experience. I mean, come on, this is far more interesting than scoring a movie that just goes unnoticed. It's a phenomenon—it's great to actually have that. I don't put it on my academic bio. I tell people about it, everybody cracks up. It's great and it's also bizarre. You have a guy with a doctorate and two masters [degrees] and all this academic stuff scoring this movie.

Are you still in touch with Tommy?
Not really. He's quite busy, and he's an iconoclastic guy. I did not socialize with him too much, but he's a little secretive . . . you cannot find out what

his background is. He has a heavy accent but he wouldn't say where he's from. He will say something completely idiotic, like he's Cajun, but I have a friend of mine who actually guessed that he may be a Turkish immigrant from Germany, so he was like listening to his accent and his facial features and said "You know what? He's a Turk whose parents immigrated from Turkey to Germany, and they came to America." It's all speculation. We don't know where Tommy's from.

Interview: Clint Jun Gamboa

Of the songs mentioned above, singer Clint Jun Gamboa sang on two of the infamous "slow jams," "Crazy" and "Baby You and Me," with Bell Johnson. After *The Room,* Clint went on to find fame as a semi-finalist on American Idol in 2011.

What was your involvement with the songs in *The Room?*
I became involved with *The Room* through a woman named Kitra Williams and her son Jarah Gibson. They are people who I consider family. Kitra is like an auntie to me, and Jarah is like a brother, or a cousin. I don't remember exactly how it all went down, but we all of a sudden were a part of this low-budget film that would go on to be this crazed phenomenon. I was pretty young when this all came about—I was about seventeen. My aunty Kitra had Tommy's contact information, and we went down one day to meet Tommy, chop it up with him about the project, sing for him in person, then—BAM!—he hired us to be a part of the soundtrack.

How was meeting Tommy? Did you know what you were letting yourself in for?
Tommy was a cool person, and you could tell that he was determined to get this movie out. No one knew the velocity of ironic success this movie would reach—at least I know I didn't. My first glimpse of this film was at the initial meeting we had with Tommy. We only saw a few clips, and of course, this was before our music was playing over the sex scenes, which by the way was a little awkward. It was kind of cool seeing it all go down at premiere of the movie.

How was that?
It actually was a fancy-schmancy event. It was still awkward, even hearing my music played on the big screen over the sex scenes. I definitely have to say that I am a fan of the film, and one of the reasons is because so many people have said that this movie was so horrible, and yet it has found success. It's a very popular movie, and I was surprised to get recognition from it.

Do you think that success will continue?
I believe this is gonna be one of those movies that MTV or VH1 talk about when they do those Top 100 Something or *I Love the 90s* type shows. You catch my drift, right? It's an honor to be a part of something with such a buzz, even if it is for peculiar reasons. I have a feeling this movie will always somewhere be talked about.

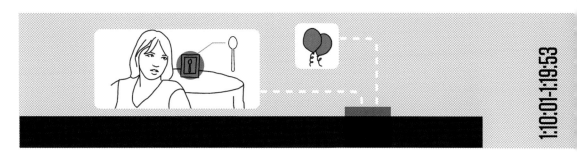

With the anticipation building as to who could be at the door, a badly dubbed (even by *The Room* standards) Lisa says, "Hurry up, I have to open the door." She and Mark make incredibly longwinded work of the deceptively simple task of putting their clothes back on, but Lisa is quickest, with Mark still topless as she giggles and tells the mystery person at the door to come in. She's seemingly forgotten that the affair is supposed to be a secret, but it's not a problem, because it's just Michelle, who takes a surprisingly laissez-faire attitude to walking in on the pair's affair, treating it with a levity that would be more fitting if Mark and Lisa were actually a couple.

"Hi, Mark. XYZ," Michelle jokes, explaining that this means "Examine your zipper." An embarrassed Mark scrambles to do up his flies as Michelle tosses the incident aside with a light "You guys are too much." Happily ignoring that fact that she has basically walked in on her best friend about to cheat on her fiancé, Michelle confirms that, outside of Denny, not a single character in this movie gives the slightest damn about Johnny. It's difficult to think of any film in which the main protagonist is so roundly dismissed and disliked by the other characters; the amount of paranoia on show from Wiseau toward his screen id would dumbfound even Freud.

Since the only reason for Mark and Lisa to interact is for sex to happen, Mark uses Michelle's intrusion as an opportunity to leave. Lisa and Michelle collapse back onto the couch, giggling like naughty schoolgirls, before we cut to a shot of Lisa asking Michelle to help her move the coffee table that was obviously filmed on a completely different day. Michelle eventually asks if Johnny knows about the affair yet, with Lisa suddenly adopting a conscience and pulling her furrowed-eyebrow "concerned" face to remind everyone that Mark is Johnny's best friend. Quite why she's gone from openly inviting whoever's at the door to walk in on her and Mark in the midst of sex to being desperate for Johnny not to know about the affair is not clear, but, you know, women, eh? Mood swings.

Wiseau chooses this point to try to give some motivation for Lisa's sudden harlotry. "You know, I really loved Johnny at first," she begins. "Everything's changed. I need more from life than what Johnny can give me. Suddenly my eyes are wide open, and I can see everything so clearly. I want it all. And if [Mark] can't give me what I want, somebody else will." So, Lisa's motivation essentially boils down to "spoiled, idiot teenager," but at least it's an attempt at giving her actions some reasoning. Michelle protests, but Wiseau clearly got bored of writing this scene, as Lisa soon resorts to her usual conversation-stopper—"I don't want to talk about it"—and gets up to empty the grocery bag on the table. She takes a seemingly number of endless packets of potato chips out of the bag, awkwardly pausing between placing each one on the table to deliver dialogue that is little more than a repeat of what she just said. "You're not such an angel yourself," she tells Michelle, with which they break into a playful, pointless pillow fight.

Next up is an astounding one minute and twenty seconds of already-used establishing shots, footage of Johnny and Mark jogging while having a conversation about loan rates that is barely audible above the music, and a ball-achingly long shot of Johnny and Mark pulling into the driveway of the townhouse. To be fair, there is at least an attempt to give this section a meaning, as shots of San Francisco at night are followed by San Francisco during the day, showing us that time has passed, but the pointless ineptitude of the whole sequence is baffling. Over an hour in, and *The Room* is still finding ways to make itself even more confusing.

It's the next morning, and Johnny, breakfast in hand, is off to work, kissing Lisa on the cheek on the way out as she pointedly stares at him with sad puppy dog eyes. It's pretty unbelievable that Johnny hasn't noticed that something's wrong, but it doesn't stop him heading out as though everything is fine. The exact second he opens the door, Claudette walks in, as though she thought it might be rude to knock, and has instead simply been standing outside the door until someone opened it to leave.

As much as we appreciate Wiseau's attempt to mix up his "every scene must start with someone entering a room" formula, this scene was clearly written to open this way because he desperately wanted Johnny to be involved in it somehow and couldn't think of any other way to do it. Barefaced narcissism, I'd say. That said, we've suffered a painful twenty-five minutes without Claudette to tide the story along, and Johnny greets her with the hug and kiss that we all want to give her, too, upon her grand return, before walking out.

Claudette—resplendent in a tasteful white suit and matching purse—struts over to Lisa and strokes her chin before taking her place on the couch. Lisa says that she's fixing up the apartment for Johnny's birthday, but she's really not into it.

Claudette asks why not, in a way that suggests she's forgotten about the revelation of Lisa's affair. A lot has happened in the last twenty-five minutes, after all—mainly establishing shots and exercise scenes, but a lot of them.

"'Cause I'm in love with Mark, not Johnny," Lisa says, for the billionth time, to which Claudette disapprovingly groans. It's interesting how Lisa mentions Mark's name this time, having pointedly failed to last time, and yet Claudette shows no surprise that it's Mark who Lisa is cheating on Johnny with. Claudette knows Mark, so why isn't she more surprised at the revelation? Has she been told already, offscreen? With no context, Claudette's reaction makes little-to-no sense, but, of course, the real reason is that the previous lack of clarity was vital to the story, as it ensured that while Johnny was aware of Lisa's betrayal, he didn't know who she was having an affair with. Here, it makes no difference, as the script only really serves to fit the contrivances of Wiseau's inane plot, and thus it doesn't matter. The sane thing to do would have been to replace one of the exercise sequences with some expository dialogue about Claudette finding out it that it's Mark—or maybe even give her a line here, in which she expresses surprise at finding out his identity—but applying "the sane thing" to *The Room* is, as always, a self-defeating experience. So we sigh, Claudette-style, and move on.

"It's not right, Lisa," Claudette says, taking Johnny's side again, having apparently forgiven him for his earlier abhorrent behavior in not

lending her best friend money. "I still think you should marry Johnny," she continues, reemphasizing his financial security. Claudette really doesn't seem to have much faith in Lisa's ability to find another man.

"But I'm not happy," Lisa barks, insisting she won't be marrying him. Claudette counters by insisting that she's not happy, either; she hasn't been happy since she was married to her first husband, and she never wanted to marry Lisa's father, either. This seems like an oddly timed and casual way to bring up such potentially life-changing news, but it gets batted away as Claudette carries on her rant on male-female relations. "All men are assholes, men and women use and abuse each other all the time, there's nothing wrong with it," she says, directly contradicting her scolding of Lisa not ten seconds earlier. "Marriage has nothing to do with love."

The Room is actually full to burst with such rampant cynicism, and the repeated clashes between this cynicism and Johnny's perpetual attempts at optimism are the emotional driving force behind the film. Here we have the two most important women in Johnny's life—his future wife and his future mother-in-law—dismissing his impending marriage as nothing more than a financial agreement, whereas Johnny continually expresses his love for Lisa and his belief in his love for her, despite the various trials and difficulties cast between them. The strength of his naivety and simple-mindedness is almost Herculean, but despite his irritating and bizarre fits of rage, it creates an underdog we care about. Johnny's optimism makes him almost too beautiful for the cynical world into which he has been cast. Unfortunately, the fact that Wiseau is writing the character as a representation of *himself* means he considers himself too beautiful for the world that we as a society have burdened him with, but let's ignore that and focus on the beauty of Johnny, truly a God among us all.

Out of the blue, Lisa decides that Johnny's OK, and that she has him wrapped around her little finger, before changing her mind again and deciding that the fact she doesn't love him is more important.

"You need to grow up," Claudette insists. "You need to listen to me."

The film cuts to a close-up of the two as they heatedly debate the issue. Lisa brushes Claudette aside: "OK, Mom, I'll see you at the party." Claudette takes the hint and leaves, with Wiseau seemingly deeming it unnecessary to offer an explanation for why she has gone around to the apartment to have the exact same conversation they've had three times already.

Next, there's a full thirty seconds of Johnny walking around San Francisco in the late evening, before we return to the darkened apartment. Somehow, the lights go on—despite the fact that Johnny hasn't touched the switch, and no one else is near one—and SURPRISE, it's Johnny's Birthday Party! The gang's all there—Denny, Mark, Lisa, Claudette, Michelle, Mike, five people we've never seen before . . . but where's Peter? Maybe his football accident eventually proved fatal. Everyone sings "Happy Birthday" to Johnny, who basks in the attention with faux-embarrassment, and they all have drinks. The previously teetotal Johnny greedily grabs at the champagne, and then the overlong clinking of glasses and meandering dialogue—clearly unscripted, or even rehearsed—plays out for the remainder of the scene.

We return with the party in full swing, generic "phat" beats playing in the background, and everyone is talking away, by all accounts having a great time—except Johnny, who, after shooting a cautionary glance as "Unnamed Guy at Party" casually flirts with Lisa, starts to fall victim to his increasing paranoia. Mark also has an eye on proceedings, as the film gradually—and, whisper it, successfully—builds up a sense of tension, with a fourth corner now seemingly trying to thrust itself into our little love triangle.

Lisa shoots Mark a glance that tells him not to worry; she only has her eye on one man tonight, and, sadly, it's not her fiancé. Oddly, the conversation between Claudette and Johnny is slightly higher in the mix than anyone else's, and we overhear Claudette pushing her friend's financial problems back onto Johnny. This is a great callback to their earlier situation, and reaffirms the fact that she is every bit as self-absorbed and selfish as her daughter—how could she bother Johnny for money at his own birthday party!? The camera pans around the room, allowing us a glimpse of Mike pulling his comic-relief faces at Michelle, before Lisa suggests that the assembled partygoers go outside for some fresh air. Despite there being only eleven people at the party, we see ten people exit the door before Lisa closes it, leaving her and Mark inside alone.

"Wait, I have something to show you," Lisa says, leading him over to the couch.

"Are you crazy?" Mark warns. "Everybody's here!"

"No, they're not. They're outside," Lisa laughs, as if she's some mastermind, ignoring the fact that anyone could come back in to use the bathroom at any given time.

"She-devil," Mark smirks, as he falls for her less-than-watertight reasoning. We are truly into the endgame now, and it's a matter of when—not if—their diabolical plans will come crashing down around them.

I feel like I'M SITTING ON AN ATOMIC BOMB WAITING FOR IT TO GO OFF.

22

You came to *The Room* late in the process, replacing Kyle Vogt's Peter. How did you first get involved with the film?

I came to be in *The Room* by way of an ad in *Backstage West,* a weekly trade paper. I can't remember now if I sent in a headshot or just went to the set directly to audition.

What were your first impressions of Tommy Wiseau, and what was it like to be directed by him?

Upon arriving on set, I was greeted by Greg Sestero, who seemed like a pleasant, professional man, and whom I assumed to be the director. I couldn't help but notice that he had brought an obviously insane, homeless crackhead onto the set and was letting this person interact with the auditions. I thought it was hilarious, and a great way to see if the actors were too uptight or could roll with it. I mentioned this to Greg, at which point he seemed very tired and said, "That's Tommy. He's the director."

This was the point at which Tommy approached me and asked if I was ready to be a movie star. He then had me act like I'd just won a million dollars. I figured I had nothing to lose, especially with a character this outrageous, so I tapped into my inner Publisher's Clearing House moment and went crazy. Tommy loved it. He immediately wanted me to make out with an actress also auditioning. This in the middle of the Birns & Sawyer parking lot in front of other actors and film crew. I was, um, OK with it, but the actress fled.

How was it fitting into a cast and crew who had already been working together for some time? How far in were they when you came on board?

I hadn't had much exposure to film sets at that time, so I couldn't really compare the *Room* experience [to anything else]. I could tell that Tommy was a really arrogant control freak who liked to yell at people. Coming in as an actor later in a film is no big deal—you figure out who people are playing, and how your character fits into the world. It was the world of the set itself that was going through trauma. I entered as the director of photography and his crew were leaving.

There was a real undercurrent of disrespect that I hadn't encountered anywhere else. I decided to have as much fun as I could, and take the checks, which I needed badly at the time. The other actors I worked with had the same kind of attitude, and we had some enjoyable times hanging out on set.

Were you given a full script, or was it explained to you how Steven fit into the story?

The only direction I ever received from Tommy was, "You are Steven. You are friend of Johnny and Lisa." I never saw an entire script, so I was free to add any kind of nuance I wanted. Basically, when I saw how awful the principle shooting looked, I didn't worry about getting an Oscar nod for this one. If anything, I tried to figure out what universe this story was taking place in, and act like the creatures who occupied it. That kind of thinking made it easier to say anything, no matter how ungrounded in natural human dialogue. The "acting" work in this was the least fun I've ever had on a job site, and I presently work in a mineral plant.

Why was that?

It's probably because I love and respect acting, and having to work for and with someone who obviously didn't know anything about it made me question my own self-esteem. The other thing is, Tommy immediately instilled in me a "fight or flight" instinct. A sickness from his very presence. It took the positive energies of every other person on the set to override my desire to either quit the film or knock him out.

Can you remember first seeing the final film, and what was that like?

I did accept the invitation for myself and my girlfriend at the time to attend the opening. We parked a block or so away from the theater on purpose, as an escape plan. I liked seeing the other people from the cast and crew, and first screenings are always exciting, but watching the film was another story. It was painful to see myself in something that bad, and I feel I mailed in a pretty crappy performance, too, but it was undeniably funny. Not just "little giggle" funny, which is how it started, but falling-out-of-your-seat hilarious—which people were doing by the end of the screening. At the end, I ran down a couple rows to where Tommy was still sitting and legitimately congratulated him. He got his movie made. That's really hard, even if you have the finances. I told him we couldn't stay for the after-party. I might have been able to for a bit, but how in the hell does one act at a party after something like that? I wish now I had gone for a bit, just to see how people handled it.

How has being in *The Room* affected your life in the last eleven years, if at all?

I successfully buried the memory of that film, and chalked it up as a learning experience. L.A. is full of people with monstrous piles of money and no ability. For $2.99, you can buy their films at the supermarket. Not being a big cult-film guy, I had no way of seeing any potential in *The Room* for what happened eventually. I had just returned from Texas, where I was production designer on an independent feature, had produced another feature for a friend, and had had a lead role in another friend's feature. This triple butt-kicking made me appreciate the effort that goes into film, [and then] I got the word about the huge explosion of popularity *The Room* experienced.

My initial reaction was the honest first reaction of anyone faced with another's success: *Fuck that asshole.* Sure, that piece of shit is funny, but . . . really? I was part of a film nominated at Sundance, which apparently wasn't crappy enough for anyone to ever see. I almost immediately mellowed my view. You know what? Good for Tommy. Let that extremely weird dude have his time. And I wish nothing but the best for Greg Sestero, one of the nicest guys you'll ever meet.

How do you feel about the cult following that has grown around *The Room,* and when did you first hear about it?

In general, I've tried not to be hypocritical about *The Room.* I didn't put it on my résumé until it was absolutely stupid not to. I've been to three public screenings, and so far have had to get pretty drunk to get through them. The first one I went to, I had to basically be carried out. The movie, to me, is basically unwatchable, and I don't like to watch myself in anything.

Why do you think *The Room* has become such a phenomenal success?

I realized that it's not about me, or "art," or any of that crap. It's about the fans and what they want. They love *The Room* and the characters in it and want a chance to show that love. It's why you come out for a curtain call. It's not for the actor. I have noticed that a lot of the fans of *The Room* are people involved in film, or film students. I think it makes it that much funnier when one can see exactly how a film is wrong.

It would take an impossible effort to intentionally make a film as bad as this. Bad films happen all the time, but not perfectly bad. There is not a single good element in it, and that makes it fascinating. If anything was even OK about it, it couldn't have caught on. It's that alternate reality where there are no rules to get in the way of pure entertainment.

LEAVE YOUR STUPID COMMENTS IN YOUR POCKET!

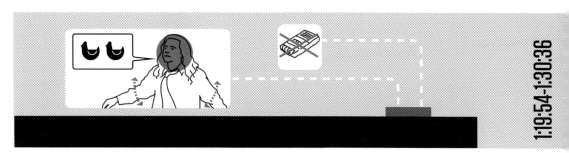

Unnamed Guy crashes the party, angrily demanding to know what's happening between Mark and Lisa. How spirit-crushingly anti-climactic, to have what should be one of the film's great dramatic moments—the big secret revealed—hung on someone with absolutely no relevance to us. Even someone with a skewed perspective should realize that Denny, the only established character with any genuine concern for Johnny at this point in the film, should have made the discovery.

At this point, it seems appropriate to mention the fact that "Unnamed Guy" does actually have a name. It's Steven, though no one calls him that in the course of the film; we know his name because there's a Steven listed in the credits, and process of elimination means it must be this guy. I'll keep referring to him as Unnamed Guy, though, because if Wiseau doesn't think he's important enough to be given a name during the film, who am I to disagree?

"Why are you doing this?" Unnamed Guy continues, awkwardly holding out his hands as though carrying an invisible pile of books, while Lisa and Mark stand there sheepishly.

"I love him," Lisa explains, holding Mark close.

"I don't believe it!" Unnamed Guy protests, before Mark explodes: "You don't understand anything, man. Leave your stupid comments in your pocket!" I'm sure Unnamed Guy would have been split to the very core by that insult—if, that is, he had even the slightest clue as to what it was supposed to mean. My guess is that Wiseau has literally translated a saying from his native tongue into English—something that never works well, and often leads to such malapropisms.

Mark, brave man that he is, storms out, leaving Lisa alone to face Unnamed Guy's ire. He stalks toward her, looking like he's ready to punch her, as the camera closes in on Lisa, trapping her in the lie of her own creation. This does serve to make us feel some sorrow for Lisa—which, given the way things have gone up to this point, is obviously not what the director was aiming for.

"You're going to destroy Johnny," Unnamed Guy warns. "He's very sensitive." Lisa just repeats her love for Mark. The drama is interrupted by Johnny and Michelle coming in. Johnny thanks Lisa (through dubbing which would have been better placed in a Godzilla movie) for the beautiful party. "You invited all my friends. Good thinking!"

"You're welcome, darling, you know how much I love you," Lisa sweetly replies, prompting an eye-rolling stare from Unnamed Guy that's so obvious that it would surely prompt even Johnny to guess something is up. In fact, given that Johnny was shooting concerned glances at Lisa and Unnamed Guy's flirting earlier in the party, shouldn't finding the two of them alone result in at least some mild questioning? Instead, yet another potentially interesting plot point is callously cast aside, as Lisa convinces everyone to simply go back outside. They do, and Johnny looks around the empty room, a look of sadness clear on his face. It could be acting, or it could be coincidence. We'll never know.

Back outside, there's a wonderfully cinematic moment as the camera tracks Lisa from behind as she walks across the roof, the party around her out of focus—we're almost tricked into thinking we're watching a real film. Unfortunately, as she exits stage right, the tracking continues, switching our focus to the permanently dim-witted Johnny, and reality hits us in the face with a wet slap. Johnny interrupts himself from waving to an invisible man outside the bottom right hand corner of the frame, and with a sudden bout of Tourette's syndrome, he shouts out, "Hey everybody! I have an announcement to make! We're expecting!"

The first person to shake Johnny's hand is Mark, who does so with his back to camera, so as to make the moment meaningless, when in fact a close-up of Mark looking concerned or shocked would have been significantly more appropriate. Instead, we get Michelle and Unnamed Guy's concerned and shocked faces as they drag Lisa to one side to question her. (No one seems interested in congratulating her on the upcoming baby.)

"You have got to be honest with Johnny," Michelle pleads.

"I agree with that," Unnamed Guy adds, for no other reason than to justify his role in the scene.

"Look, I'm gonna tell him," Lisa says. "I just . . . I don't want to ruin his birthday," she adds, nervously playing with her fingers at the increasing realization that she's running out of excuses to keep this whole thing a secret.

"When is . . . the baby . . . due," Unnamed Guy asks, with all the passion and intonation you'd expect if Stephen Hawking had been his line-reading coach.

126

"There is no baby," Lisa replies. "I told him that to make it interesting." She then tries to justify the stupidity of every single aspect of that statement by adding, "We're probably going to have a baby eventually anyway."

OK, let's take this one step at a time, Lisa:

1) How are you going to explain to Johnny that you haven't put on any weight during your "pregnancy"—or that, in nine months' time, there's no baby?
2) You've spent the last eighty minutes telling anyone who'll listen that you have no intention of marrying Johnny and want to leave him. How exactly does having a baby together fit into this?
3) Don't you love Mark? How will Mark feel about the woman who loves him procreating with someone else?

"Lisa, are you feeling OK?" Michelle asks, jokingly holding her hand against Lisa's head in a moment of completely inappropriate frivolity.

"I feel like I'm sitting on an atomic bomb waiting for it to go off," Unnamed Guy adds, though the camera isn't pointing at him, as instead we're watching Lisa as she grimaces at the taste of some flat champagne.

"Me too," Michelle agrees. "There's no simple solution to this." Yes, there is. Break up with Johnny and tell him you've been lying. It's not nice, but it's as simple as it gets.

Lisa tells them not to worry, but Michelle, rather callously, replies that they're not worried about her—they're worried about Johnny. This being the same Michelle who smiled excitedly when she found out Lisa was having the affair in the first place.

"You don't understand the psychological impact of what you're doing here . . . you're hurting our friendship," Michelle continues, prompting Lisa to reply, "I'm not responsible for Johnny, I'm through with that!" Clearly she's changed her stance on having a baby with him. She carries on with a typical rant that shows just how much scorn the script has for women, before Unnamed Guy drops the bombshell that he thinks Mark doesn't really love her. Now, we're not sure what Unnamed Guy is basing this on, given that his entire discussion with Mark about this concerned where his comments should be kept, but this omnipotent insight proves too much for Lisa, who (uncharacteristically) doesn't want to talk about it, and instead gets up to order everyone in from the balcony for cake.

If there's one thing that's been missing from the script recently, it's a reference to how attractive Lisa is. Noticing that gap in the market, Another Man at the Party takes his stab at immortality by deciding to tell his significant other that "Lisa looks hot tonight." She is, understandably, a little put out at this statement, and as she questions him about it, the camera pans down to a conversation between Claudette and Johnny, who seem to be spending a lot of time together. The two conversations overlap in the sound mix, and we can't really hear either of them.

Mark's initial excitement at Lisa's pregnancy seems to have gone, as he suddenly realizes that babies come from sex and, given the amount of sex the two have had recently, there's a chance the baby might be his. He decides to interrogate Lisa about this in the middle of the party, prompting her to angrily slap him in front of everyone. Perhaps not the best way to draw attention away from your illicit dealings, but then Wiseau's script has gone to excessive lengths in the last few scenes to paint Lisa as someone with the emotional maturity of a thirteen-year-old, so she may as well possess the common sense of one, too.

Johnny runs over to quell the anger and ask what's going on. "You really don't know, do you?" Mark taunts. Johnny somehow puts two and two together—despite the fact that all the evidence he has about Lisa's betrayal points more toward Unnamed Guy—and strikes out at Mark. A simple one-handed push somehow catapults Mark across the room, leading him to crash into a table, and the two break out into a fight. The guests break it up; Johnny gallantly apologizes to everyone and offers Mark his hand. Johnny then asks Lisa to tidy up the mess, walks off, and . . . stands behind the kitchen door. Hmm.

With all eyes on Mark and Lisa, what would the sensible thing be for the pair to do? Talk cordially, but maintain a respectable distance? Not speak to each other at all? How about dancing in the middle of the party, and make motions at kissing each other on the neck? Of course, it's the latter. Johnny comes out from behind the door to ask Lisa what she's doing. Mark tells him to leave her alone, prompting Johnny to aim a shove at Mark's chest, and the two once again square up.

"What planet are you on?" Mark asks—a phrase we suspect Wiseau has heard more than once in his life.

"I think you should leave right now, Mark," Johnny replies, displaying reasonable restraint by his standards. Mark offers a comforting pat on the arm, which proves too much for Johnny. "Don't touch me, muuuuttthhafaarkkkaaagetooouut," he slurs, the anger severing the link between his brain and his voice box. Another fight breaks out, and Johnny's incredible pushing strength once again leaves Mark on his ass across the other side of the room.

"You're going to ruin the party!" Lisa pleads—seemingly believing a party that has already seen two fights break out in it is not yet beyond redemption. Johnny ignores her plea, removing his jacket and launching at Mark, belligerently yelling unintelligible threats. Once again, the fight is broken up before it gets too nasty, but Johnny can't leave things alone this time. "You betrayed me, you're not good. You . . . you're just a chicken!" he spits out, remolding his greasy locks before adopting the now familiar mocking pose of flapping arms and chirping noises, clearly not understanding that it makes him look far more ridiculous than the person it's aimed at. Mark goes in for one last scuffle, but Unnamed Guy breaks it up, yelling, "It's over."

Johnny, once again, must have the last word. "It's not over. Everybody betrayed me. I'm fed up with this world," he says, adding emphasis to the word "world" by saying it in a lower octave than the rest of the sentence. He then ambles pathetically upstairs as we try to reconcile the strange combination of pity, disgust, embarrassment, and amusement that the whole pathetic revelation of Lisa and Mark's forbidden trysts has caused—the emotional fulcrum of the entire film boiled down to an unsatisfying and embarrassing parade of confusing logic, misuse of characters, feeble acting, and cheeping.

An establishing night shot of San Francisco's Disney Store is our only visual clue to the passing of time as we transition to upstairs after the party. Claudette is comforting Lisa with the news that the kitchen is clean. Lisa is worried about Johnny hiding in the bathroom, but Claudette tells her that'll he calm down eventually, before leaving to give them the chance to talk alone. Sadly, that is the last we see of Claudette, the character who so wonderfully strode the fine line between Wiseau's desire for someone to espouse Johnny's good points and his need to adhere to the "fact" that all women are conniving, selfish bitches.

Pondering her next move in the game of mental chess that is interacting with Johnny, Lisa awkwardly paces around the bedroom, stopping only to try to open the bathroom door.

"You can come out now, Johnny, she's gone," Lisa says, as though Johnny was hiding from Claudette, and not her.

"In a few minutes, bitch," Johnny huffs.

Bizarrely, Lisa then asks who the bitch is, and even more bizarrely, Johnny replies, "You and your stupid mother," which doesn't really match the context of the exchange at all. The slight on her mother proving too much, Lisa grabs for the phone to call Mark. Johnny tries his best to listen in on the conversation through the door as Lisa and Mark trade their stock "I want you" lines.

Johnny exits the bathroom, demanding to know whom Lisa was talking to. When she refuses to tell him, he closes the bathroom door— twice—and says, "We'll see about that!" before disappearing downstairs and then returning with . . . the tape! Anyone would be forgiven for having forgotten about this particular plot device—the tape machine having been introduced over forty minutes ago, and never referenced again— but it will play its part in the conclusion.

Johnny shakes the tape at Lisa, who of course has no idea what it is or what he aims to prove with it. Wiseau apparently forgets what part of the script they've reached, repeats the words "We'll see about that," and plays the tape.

Now, the amount of magical things about Johnny's tape machine are numerous, but the most notable must be the fact that, despite having been attached to the phone for several days, it seems to have recorded only the ONE message appropriate to making his point. On top of that, it has conveniently rewound to the exact start of that conversation, so Johnny doesn't have to do anything more than press play. There's a common misconception that the dialogue on the tape doesn't match that of the actual conversation, but that's not true—it actually just includes the lines that we didn't hear, because the camera cut away to Johnny eavesdropping through the door. (There's already enough material to use against this movie—you don't need to make stuff up.)

As his world comes crashing down around him, Johnny stops the tape to air his frustrations at Lisa, hamming it up as only Wiseau can, his intonation and voice pitch fluctuating like a pin on a lie detector test. "How could you duuuuuueeeeewwww this to me?" he hollers. Reaching the end of the taped conversation, Johnny explodes and hurls the tape recorder against the wall; it simply makes a rather disappointing thud as it drops on the stairs, instead of shattering into a million pieces. Seems Johnny's pushing is stronger than his throwing.

"Everybody betrayed me, I don't have a friend in the world," Johnny says, falling to the bed and wallowing in his oft-repeated self-pity. Lisa takes one last look at him before uttering the inevitable "I'm leaving you, Johnny" and walking out of his life forever.

24

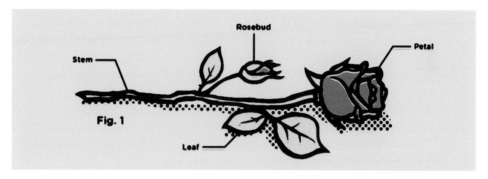

Take a deep breath, clear your mind, and open yourself up to the possibility that maybe, just maybe, *The Room* is not the *"Citizen Kane of bad movies"*[1] but actually the twenty-first-century *Citizen Kane;* that Tommy Wiseau is the new Orson Welles. Now, you may have just spat coffee all over the page, but hear me out.

Let's consider the facts. Orson Welles was able to produce his debut feature film *Citizen Kane* with the freedom of total creative control, owing to the success of his earlier works in other areas, including the RKO radio production of *War of the Worlds*.[2] Does that sound like someone we know? Of course, you may wish to point out that Welles was artistically successful, as well as commercially, but you'd be overlooking the fact that, as well as having the entrepreneurial smarts to make enough money out of his own businesses to have total creative control over *The Room,* Wiseau did get an A- for his film-school short *Robbery Doesn't Pay.*[3]

It's no wonder, then, that with *The Room,* Wiseau was poised to follow in the footsteps of Welles and reinvent cinema. It's well documented that his film, like *Citizen Kane,* invented its own language. Whereas Welles and Gregg Toland pioneered deep-focus photography,[4] Wiseau and Todd Baron revolutionized the use of extremely shallow or "out of focus" photography, as it has become known. Consider the way he shot the film in two formats, and other innovations such as the combo-language subtitles option on the Blu-ray release—evidence, perhaps, of a forward thinking of a genius ahead of his time. Welles may have pioneered the use of low angles to show ceilings, but where Wiseau was going, he didn't need ceilings.

Of course, it is on the record that *Citizen Kane* is Tommy Wiseau's favorite film,[5] and aside from the "bedroom-smashing" scene, these films share a number of similarities. As Wiseau himself put it, "The movie, it's dealing with the relationships, dealing with the business . . . what is behind the works? Politics, etc. etc. So, I strongly recommend this movie because it have everything in it, from love to hatred . . . it's the same like *The Room*."[6]

See, on the surface, the film is about a self-made wealthy businessman who made his own fortune out of nothing and fell in love with a beautiful woman, only to see the relationship unravel under the weight of an affair. Eventually, he dies unloved. That's Charles Foster Kane, not Johnny. Looking deeper, both films study what it is to be loved, to be truly happy and the loss of innocence. Finally then, think about the autobiographical nature of *The Room* and the mystery of Wiseau's past, and perhaps look upon a lost childhood and the sense of a young boy corrupted by the world. Next time you watch *The Room,* pour yourself a Scotchka and look a little deeper into it, and maybe, just maybe, there is something within that dozen red roses—the "Rosebud"—a single key that unlocks the secret of the auteur's past, his origin, and his heart.

So, the moment we've all been waiting for has finally happened, and now we ponder where next Wiseau will take this story. What Johnny thought was his perfect life has been ripped apart before his very eyes, and now he sits wondering what is happening, before going over to the staircase, casually leaning on it, and shouting, "Get out, get out, get out of my life!" This would certainly have had more impact if Lisa had been there to hear him say it, but we guess we can accept it, as long as it is cathartic for Johnny. (Incidentally, has Johnny forgotten that Lisa's supposedly pregnant? He seems pretty unconcerned that his unborn child has gone, along with its mother. Maybe he was just feigning excitement.)

Johnny ambles downstairs, drops into his armchair, and has flashbacks of all the good times he had with Lisa, while pulling faces that resemble a cross between anger and a reaction to having his chest waxed. Then, having sat down for long enough, Johnny decides that this situation calls for action, and that the only mature and responsible way to deal with his emotion is to go on an Incredible Hulk–esque rampage throughout his home. In one of the most passionless displays of cathartic destruction imaginable, Johnny ambles around his apartment, emitting oddly misplaced grunts of frustration, in between which he reverts to his standard vacant, lobotomy-patient stare. His particular method of destruction could loosely be described as "vaguely swiping at things and seeing if they fall over," but he does later branch out into throwing an (unplugged) TV out of the window, with an exterior shot following of the TV crashing to the ground outside in broad daylight, even though it should be nighttime. Johnny then wanders upstairs to carry on the destruction, which includes a limp pushing over of a dresser, while hollering his best impersonation of Timmy from *South Park*.

Eventually, his rage sated, he sits down and decides it's time to satisfy another basic need. Cue Johnny sniffing Lisa's dress and rubbing it down his body before, for all intents and purposes, masturbating with it. This is intercut with shots of Lisa naked—because we haven't already been seen enough of that in the movie. These intercuts of paradise soon change to paradise lost, causing Johnny to tear the dress apart in a rage. Yes, the dress that symbolized his love for Lisa at the start of the film is now torn apart, telling us that this really is the end of their relationship.

What now for Johnny? Surely the only way to end this film is to have him rise phoenix-like from the flames and overcome adversity. For Wiseau, someone so clearly steeped in Americana, this should surely be a tale of strength against the odds. After all, this is Johnny's story, and everything we know about Johnny points to him being the eternal optimist. The best revenge is living well and . . . oh wait, he's got a gun. A gun? Where's that come from? Some fans of The Room suggest the gun is Chris-R's, but there's no point where Johnny could have gotten it from Chris-R, given that it was Mark who grabbed the gun from him, after which they wrestled Chris-R to the police station with the weapon firmly against his head; plus it's safe to assume that the police probably took the gun as evidence. There's also the fact it *looks* different, of course, if we want to get technical about such matters.

Casually reaching for a box and taking the gun out like it was part of his plan all along, Johnny gingerly toys with the firearm, pondering the enormity of what he's thinking of doing next. "Why? Why is this happening to . . . why? It's over," he bleats, with all the emotional range that a man who cannot act in any way, shape, or form can muster. Finally, the camera zooms in close on Johnny's profile as he pleads for God's forgiveness and puts the gun in his mouth, his last thoughts being of Lisa telling him everything will be all right, before pulling the trigger and ending the tale of Johnny, once and for all. The world goes into slow motion as Johnny falls back and the gun falls to the floor, the sound of the gunshot echoing into a profound silence.

It's a beautiful ending . . . except it isn't the ending, because now we must suffer a coda that shows how sad everyone is that Johnny's dead, because he was, after all, the greatest man who ever lived. Having heard the gunshot, Mark and Lisa come hurtling in and fall by Johnny's side. With a huge pool of blood having formed and dried around his head—and somehow managed to run onto the front of his shirt, despite the fact it would have been impossible for it to get there—it's clearly game over for Johnny, but Mark still won't give up on him.

"Wake up, Johnny, come on!" he pleads. Lisa is similarly lacking in the "big pond of blood gushing out of your head means you're dead" department, asking, "Is he dead? My God, Mark, is he dead?" This isn't a rhetorical question; Lisa genuinely seems to think that a gunshot to the head is something Johnny might have survived. After getting some comically fake-looking blood on his hands, Dr. Mark eventually declares the patient dead. There's tears and remorse all round, as the camera focuses once too often on Johnny, who, even in death, has to be the most visible character in any given scene.

"I've lost him, but I still have you, right?" Lisa asks, conveniently forgetting she had left Johnny so no longer had him to lose. Angered by her self-absorption in the face of the death of his friend, Mark pushes her away, telling her that she killed Johnny. "Get out of my life, you bitch!" he yells, pushing her so hard she goes out of focus. Luckily, she returns to focus just in time to see Denny rushing in—apparently, it took him around a minute or two longer than Mark and Lisa to realize that a gunshot from Johnny's place might be a bad noise. As Denny scrambles to get to Johnny's body, he orders the others away, all too aware that their actions have led to the death of his surrogate father. Taking the chance to make one more nonsensical comment with no immediate context ("As far as I'm concerned, you can drop off the face of the earth. That's a promise."), Mark storms out, yelling for Lisa to follow him, leaving Denny alone with the corpse.

"Why, Johnny? Why?" Denny pleads, not knowing he is the answer to his own question: if you were so unpopular, your death was only going to be mourned by one person, and that person was Denny, wouldn't you kill yourself, too? Lisa and Mark look back on Denny's tears, but they look sadder that Denny is upset rather than concerned for the fact that Johnny's

brain fluid is currently seeping over the bedroom floor. They go back to comforting him as police sirens and indistinct voices chatter nonsensically over one final shot of Johnny lying on the floor, his arms spread wide, as though he was crucified, while Denny, Mark, and Lisa cry around his body. Johnny died for our sins—our sins being that we didn't want to spend time with a bizarrely accented, disturbed, greasy-haired, cheeping goofball with a penchant for trying to have sex with women's navels.

Finally, we fade to black and into the credits. In one last bizarre twist, as we exit the theater sadly considering the death of the innocent Johnny, the soundtrack cuts from a mere thirteen seconds of doleful music to "You Are My Rose," which was last heard during Mark and Lisa's first sex scene. What, given this association, are we to assume is happening after the film has faded away from the scene of Johnny's death? The only thing I can think of is that the film does indeed have a happy ending, and Denny did get his threesome, after all.

And there we have it: *The Room,* a ninety-nine-minute morality play–cum–unintentional black comedy about betrayal, set against a backdrop of unbelievable characters doing unbelievable things for reasons that no one with a basic grasp of human behavior would ever consider relatable. Regardless of whether you were at the film's L.A. premiere in 2003 or are starting your journey into the Wiseauverse with this book, what you are witnessing is clearly the work of a man who mixes an incredible lack of talent with a sense of self-obsession that hasn't tipped into self-awareness. Using this unique combination, he made a movie in which he tries to get over a broken heart by blaming every single person in the world—except himself.

In writing this, I've come to realize even more fully how bad *The Room* is. Usually, in examining something in such detail, you start to find little nuggets of quality, but if anything, my opinion of the film's technical merits is now even lower than it was when I started. Yet I don't hate *The Room* the way I do, say, *Transformers: Revenge of the Fallen* or *Star Wars Episode II: Attack of the Clones.* Nobody hates *The Room.* To hate it is impossible, even mean-spirited—it's a misguided, unintelligent child who wears its heart so openly upon its sleeve as to become lovable. It's something to be celebrated.

Why does this kind of film inspire such attention, when films of genuine quality are so regularly ignored? Why aren't you reading a book about Wong Kar Wai's *In the Mood for Love?* Why am I not writing 25,000 words about *Mulholland Drive* or analyzing the motivations of Daniel Plainview in *There Will Be Blood?* What does this say about us, as twenty-first-century moviegoers? Our whole relationship with film stems almost solely from our understanding of how great films work. Whether it be Truffaut's legendary interviews with Alfred Hitchcock[1] or more recent works such as Geoff Dyer's study of Tarkovsky's *Stalker* in

Zona,[2] truly great film theory has often interpreted cinema as a malleable concept, acting as a mirror not only to its creator but also to us, as a way to purely reflect upon ourselves. By analyzing man's cinematic accomplishments, we focus clearly on the good that mankind—and, by extension, we ourselves—can achieve.

But how can we understand the good if we don't truly understand the bad? Clarity can only be achieved through a true grasp of the darkness that resides not only with cinema, but also within us. *The Room* is the very paradigm of this sheer incompetence. Sometimes, we can only recognize beauty when faced so brazenly with darkness. Wiseau—and those who made up his motley crew of people who don't understand how to act, dub, manage continuity, use a green screen, track a camera properly, or any other of the basic things associated with recording moving images—have inadvertently defined a new strand of cinema: *anti*-cinema, a type of cinema that presents us so succinctly with what not to do as to serve to reinforce how lucky we are to have the works of an Orson Welles, Alfred Hitchcock, or Martin Scorsese.

The Room is our collective route into that darkness. For all the ironic love bestowed upon it, for every *Rocky Horror*-esque crowd-participation screening, its true role is as a way to explore our love of cinema through looking directly at the exact opposite of what we think cinema is and can be. As we slowly realize the importance of *The Room,* what does the future hold for it? Just take Johnny's advice, and remember: don't plan too far ahead; it may not turn out right.

* * *

Alan Jones is an English teacher in Kyoto City, Japan. His relationship with *The Room* began in 2008, the obsession blooming after he arrived in Japan in 2010 with no Internet, limited Japanese, and only the film on his hard drive to while away the evenings. This is Alan's first published work, and is a long way from his MA thesis on modernity and femininity in Japanese cinema.

PART THREE

"OBSESSION"

LIFE OUTSIDE *THE ROOM*

26

Tommy Wiseau followed the lengthy process of writing, producing, directing, and starring in *The Room* by carrying the film through post-production and independently financing its marketing, distribution, and exhibition. Eventually, the cult following grew, and the film began to finance itself in L.A.—and, later, around the world. As any fan will testify, much of Wiseau's time since then has been consumed with touring the film and making personal appearances across the globe.

The impact of carrying this huge project to fruition and eventual success has meant that Wiseau is indelibly linked to *The Room.* Aside from an unseen Super 8 short entitled *Robbery Doesn't Pay,* which he has only referenced since finding fame,[1] the film was his directorial debut; as such, little to nothing was known of what future projects this mysterious auteur could conceive. Despite this, his decision to follow a personal melodrama and/or black comedy with an independently produced documentary about homelessness in L.A. was probably not something early adopters of *The Room* would have predicted.

Homeless in America (Wiseau/Redford, 2004)

In 2004, Wiseau conceived of the twenty-nine minute *Homeless in America,* which he co-directed along with Kaya Redford. Redford also assumes the role of the main interviewer throughout the film. Looking somewhat like an all-American, blonde version of Tommy, he talks with people living on the streets and other members of the community about the growing problem of homelessness in L.A. and across America. The interviews themselves are frank and often compelling, although the production values and the structuring of the film let down what could have been a valuable piece of work. Personnel from *The Room* returned to work on the documentary, including editor Eric Yalkut Chase, director of photography Todd Barron, and soundman Zsolt Magyar, which is perhaps where the problem lies; the footage used is occasionally shaky and of poor quality, and is edited together in a manner that sees shots repeated and the message of the film rendered unclear, and even the end credits appear prematurely for a frame.

Homeless in America is another example of an obviously sincere project that, while admittedly powerful in parts, falls wide of the mark required for it to have the intended impact. These problems of audiovisual quality and structure aside, the film is also an awkward length; it's too short to be a feature film but longer than the average short. This problem was heightened by the film's distribution. It is currently only available on a DVD produced by Wiseau-Films. The disc doesn't even offer so much as a menu—something that might be ignored if the profits were contributed to a homeless charity, but they're not. The project would almost certainly work to raise awareness about the problem better if it were made available for free online viewing, which might also offset suspicion aroused by the envelope enclosed with the DVD, addressed to Wiseau-Films and requesting monetary donations for a future project— which is yet to appear, ten years later. *Room* fans curious to see Wiseau will catch only a couple of brief glimpses, and even these are sometimes only in reflections. As such, the film is best recommended for educational purposes only.

The Neighbors (Wiseau/Kong, 2007–2014?)

Wiseau's first major project following *The Room* was a sitcom he wrote and created called *The Neighbors,* with an as-yet-unreleased twenty-two minute pilot episode shot in the spring of 2007. Since then, not much has come to light about the project, although an official website was established at www.theneighborssitcom.com, which lay largely dormant until July 2014 when the project was relaunched.

The 2007 pilot itself revolves around the office of a man named Charlie (Wiseau), a building manager with an open door who is faced with the varying problems of his "zany" tenants. The episode is made up of meandering, semi-improvised scenes, edited together in a seemingly random fashion, with some scenes repeating, and events occurring in the wrong order. The dysfunctional tenants gather to welcome the arrival of the mysterious Princess Penelope to America, and the episode culminates with a surprise birthday party for Charlie's secretary/partner Bebe, which descends into male stripping and a cake fight.

Unexpectedly, more footage emerged in 2011 via the Wiseau-Films official YouTube channel[2] with a short, low-quality video simply entitled "neighbors.mov," the release of which might have been an attempt to resurrect the project. The footage shows partly improvised rehearsal footage for the pilot shot by cast member Branden Kong and Wiseau himself in July/August 2005. In the style of *The Room* auditions, most of the scenes shown take place outside, having been shot in San Francisco's Japanese Tea Garden. The rehearsals include discussions of a dead cat in a washing machine, debate over whether Princess Penelope is actually called "Peanut Butter," a mention of Charlie's girlfriend "Lisa," and a basketball being tossed around, plus there's an "Oh hai, Annie!" thrown in for good measure.

At the time of writing, *The Neighbors* is still in production, and is being rebooted at the hands of Branden Kong, who has now assumed more of a creative role on the 2014 production, which is now mooted for a September release and from the two short trailers released thus far, bares little resemblance to the 2007 pilot. What follows is a discussion with Kong about *The Neighbors* and a short interview with cast member Jennifer Lieberman.

Interview: Branden Weslee Kong, Director/Writer/Producer/Star of *The Neighbors*

Can you tell me how *The Neighbors* got started?
Tommy Wiseau is the creator of the show and had the idea back in 2003 after the release of *The Room*. We filmed the first *Neighbors* pilot back in 2007, and that version didn't come out right, so we killed the project and left it for dead. Soon after, Tommy became more popular, and his popularity became marketable. The night Greg Sestero's book *The Disaster Artist* came out, Tommy and I talked about re-doing *The Neighbors*, but this time with me in charge. He agreed, and gave me until May 1, 2014, to finish the production,[3] but only a month to come out with a script. I wrote this to be the same story as the first one, but with different types of characters, and I cleaned up a lot of the continuity errors in his original story. I took away some of Tommy's magic from the first story but added my own scenes to help support the idea of his creation.

Tell me a little bit about the new version of *The Neighbors*. What's the show about, and what can we expect from it?
The backstories of the tenants are the main stories in each episode, focusing on how Charlie needs to help each neighbor out. This story takes place in the same universe as *The Room*—there are a lot of references to it in episode one, and in every episode after that there is at least one reference to it. The references are so discreet that not even the biggest *Room* fan will pick it up—not even Tommy. He doesn't want it to be in the same universe, but some of these references would actually answer some crazy questions about *The Room*.

The world has been waiting for some time now, with the original trailer clocking 369,000 views on YouTube since 2009. What's the reason for the delay?
The original is so terrible that it shouldn't be seen in the light of day. I have shown it to some friends, and they wish they could un-see it. The

delay is that there was no motivation to make this show anymore, but after Greg's book, Tommy and I said we will attempt the project one last time. The problem with the first project was that I wasn't there to help him. Now that I can get to L.A., we can make this project together.

From what I understand, you're co-directing *The Neighbors* with Tommy. What has that relationship been like?
Tommy is the main director of the show. I am only behind the camera when Tommy is in the scene, and he will be saying cut whenever he feels like. I try to get the shots done while Tommy puts his magic in. When the scenes are with the other actors, I try to direct, because I have the vision on how I want them, and Tommy steps aside because he trusts my judgment. It has been a very long process, because I have to work around Tommy's *Room* tour schedule and hold back filming until he comes back to L.A. to shoot.

Where/when can we expect to see the show? Do you have a distribution deal, or it will be another independent release from Wiseau-Films?
We will have a teaser at WonderCon 2014—maybe we might show the first episode, but we are only showing at our booth. There's no distribution deal yet. We still need to see how popular this project becomes.

Lastly, do you think *The Neighbors* will have the same impact as *The Room*?
I don't think it will have the same type of impact. This is basically a project that the Tommy fans will want to see. The fans want to see a TV show version of *The Room,* with Tommy acting and not playing himself, and watching him as a sitcom character.

Interview: Jennifer Lieberman, Actress in *The Neighbors*

How did you become involved in the project, and what was the casting process like?
I had just moved to L.A. from New York—I don't even think I was in town two months. I answered a casting notice in *Backstage* magazine and was offered an audition. The casting process was interesting. Several actors were invited to Tommy's studio to improvise some scenes; no script, no character description. We had to come to the "office" with a problem about our apartment. It reminded me of a Meisner training exercise. Some of us were asked to come back. We rehearsed one to two times per week for almost two months or so. The rehearsals were a revolving door of cast members coming and going. I guess because I come from a theater background, the development and rehearsals were fun for me, and I was happy to stick around and see how it played out.

You play Jen. Did you develop the character, and is she is based on you?
In the original pilot, my character's name is Mariana, and I developed that entire character. The first pilot was created through a group of actors doing improvisation with characters and stories we each came up with on our own. Of course, Tommy had to like and agree with what we were doing, but that initial pilot was a collaboration of all the artists involved. The character Jen in the current incarnation of the project is indeed named after me. She has the same role/story as Mariana, just a different name.

Why has *The Neighbors* been delayed for so long?
I'm not involved in the production side, so I don't know what the story is. In 2011, Tommy called me to shoot a couple more scenes for the show. I was the only one from the original cast there. This time, Greg Sestero was also there, and I got to work with both him and Tommy. I don't know what happened with that footage. Maybe they were using it to shop the project around.

How was it to work with Tommy?
Tommy was a lot of fun to work with. He gave us all plenty of room to create and play, which really facilitated our ability to bring some crazy characters and physical comedy to life. I truly look forward to working with him again. I must admit, though, he did have the cast go outside and toss a football around while improvising lines.

The House That Drips Blood on Alex (Richard/LaBorde, 2010)

Aside from a small role as a doctor in the second episode of *Playboy Adventures* in 2006, Tommy Wiseau's first major post-*Room* appearance was as himself in the fourth season of the comedy series *Tim and Eric Awesome Show, Great Job!*, which aired on Adult Swim in March 2009. In an episode simply titled "Tommy," Wiseau "guest-directs" and takes control of turning the duo's character Pigman into a feature film, casting himself as the lead alongside Jessica Alba . . . although it's not *the* Jessica Alba. The episode pokes fun at Wiseau and features clips of *The Room*, lovingly parodying it by having the set and style of *Pigman* feature some of its most recognizable characteristics, including the music, set design, and the listing of Wiseau's name several times over the opening credits.

The 2010 short film *The House that Drips Blood on Alex (THTDBOA)* was the first significant release to show Wiseau playing a character not based on himself or his increasingly notorious public persona. The comedy/horror short sees him play Alex, a "young" man who signs the deed for a mysterious house on Blood Street. After he moves in, the house begins to drip blood from the ceiling—and only on him. The rest of the film focuses on the unraveling of this mystery. The short perfectly balances Wiseau's natural comic talents with an interesting story, and is certainly one of his best projects, outside of *The Room.*

Interview: Brock LaBorde, Director of *THTDBOA* and Producer of *The Tommy Wi-Show*

How did you come to work with Tommy Wiseau?

I ask myself this question every morning. Long story short, my amazing manager Danielle Robinson contacted Tommy out of the blue and got me a meeting with him, because she knew I was such a big, instant fan of *The Room*. That wound up being one of the most bizarre, two-hour meetings of my life. Tommy seemed a little guarded and wary of me at first, and I could tell that he had probably met a lot of crummy people who mistreated and/or misunderstood him. I'm not claiming to totally understand the brain of Tommy Wiseau—that's impossible, even for Tommy—but I think that we recognized some sort of strange artistic kinship in each other; we're both self-taught filmmakers who came to L.A. with virtually no industry contacts and lots of crazy ideas. Magically, by the end of that meeting, Tommy loosened up and told me that he really wanted to figure out something for us to work on together. I left the office in a daze, not knowing what the hell I was going to do with him, but I wanted nothing else in life but to figure that out as soon as possible.

What inspired *THTDBOA*, and did you always have Tommy in mind for it?
Oddly enough, I wrote *THTDBOA* with my buddy Jared Richard back in 2004, while we still lived in New Orleans. It was a twelve-page stupid horror short that we actually filmed half of before Hurricane Katrina kicked us out to L.A. Basically, we just wanted to write a purposefully dumpy, non-scary horror film that we could easily produce. The guy who played Alex in that version was a local Louisiana actor named Andrew Evans, and he perfectly embodied the aloof protagonist that we wanted to see: somebody who plods through a horror movie without really understanding that he's in a horror movie until he stumbles across his own dead body in his attic. So stupid.

After my first meeting with Tommy, I went home and asked all my comedy buds what we were going to do, and somehow we remembered our unfinished masterpiece, *THTDBOA*, and [were] knocked out by how perfect it was. We had somehow written the dorkiest dialogue that would sound perfect coming out of Tommy's mouth. So we didn't change a word of it, and I immediately emailed a contact at Comedy Central and pitched him the idea as a one-off stupid horror short, with Tommy as the lead. He loved it, and then I sent the script to Tommy, really hoping that he'd like it. He did. Then Tommy and I went to a meeting with about a dozen Comedy Central people, and they started it off by asking me if I was interested in turning *THTDBOA* into a TV series.

After shitting my pants with excitement, I pitched them a *Tales from the Crypt*–like dumb horror anthology show, with Tommy as the crypt-keeper storyteller, and they said *THTDBOA* could be a test pilot of sorts for it. Aside from Tommy, I wanted to pepper in all sorts of cool actors from really different projects, which is why I cast Joey Greco from TV's *Cheaters* and online video stars like iJustine and Brookers. Basically, the show would be a celebration of talented people that I thought didn't get the kind of recognition they deserved.

Of course, Tommy took this opportunity to completely derail the meeting by sliding DVDs of his self-produced sitcom *The Neighbors* across the table and asking if they'd be interested in broadcasting that show, with me attached as a writer/producer. I had to clear the air and tell everyone that we had never discussed this, and that while I wasn't opposed to the idea, I was in no way attached to *The Neighbors* at that point. Everyone laughed, but I'm sure they were weirded out. After, I had to explain to Tommy that you can't pitch a series to a network while they're trying to hand you another series. He didn't get it, and still doesn't, but that's OK, because he's Tommy Wiseau.

So, Comedy Central gave us a super-tiny budget, and we shot *THTDBOA* on a RED camera and then debuted it at Comic-Con in front of a sold-out room of 1,000 wild TW fans. Since it was the first real thing for Tommy to do after *The Room,* we got a TON of press from it. Nobody had seen more than a second of the short by then, including Tommy, so that was personally one of my favorite moments in life: watching Tommy and a room full of his fans watching a weird new thing with him in it.

The series never ended up happening, because that division of Comedy Central folded soon after, but I've written follow-up episodes—the series is called *Untold Tales*—and Tommy calls me all the time asking when we're going to shoot them. Gosh, if I had an extra $100k lying around, I'd do it in a heartbeat.

Tommy is quite notorious for his interest in vampires, and perhaps thinks himself to be one. Did this feed into the film, or Tommy's involvement with it?

Well, there's not one mention or hint of vampirism in *THTDBOA,* although there is a skeleton and some blood, so maybe you could read some vampiric undertones in there.[4] During shooting, Tommy told me he had some theories about Alex being a vampire, and on multiple occasions, he pitched me ideas for a sequel, which involved Alex coming back to life as the King of Vampires, driving a convertible Porsche that flies and having beautiful women on his arms.[5] For the first year and a half that I knew Tommy, I never saw him consume food of any sort. He drank Red Bull on set, and once, he dumped a packet of Emergen-C down his throat, choking it down dry. On set, he semi-jokingly tried to bite two of our actors and a couple of crew members. But that's just his sense of humor.

I took some inspiration from him and wrote an episode of *Untold Tales* called "Down for the Count," which was about an immortal vampire boxer named Count Drakul who was undefeated for centuries because he would always draw first blood from his opponents and then rip them apart. Tommy would've played Drakul, and I was hoping to have Greg Sestero be his opponent hero. I even had Dave Coulier attached to be the boxing coach in that one. It was gonna be absolutely bonkers, but then the project never happened.

You're in a small club of people to have directed Tommy. What's it like?

Tommy is a blast to direct. He tends to focus less on things like recalling the dialogue as written, or hitting his mark, and instead tries to get the right kind of energy out of the scene. He really pushes his fellow actors to give him as much as he's giving to them. It's really fun to watch. He's very respectful of everyone, and I never experienced him being ill-tempered or anything. He's especially sweet around any sort of ladies that are around—actresses, makeup people, and assistants. He's kind of chivalrous, in a way. I hope he finds a nice girl and settles down one day.

Sure, you do have to deal with all sorts of idiosyncrasies from Tommy along the way—he will only show up to set after a certain time of the day—but overall, he's pretty easygoing once he knows and trusts you, and I never felt like he was difficult or impossible to direct. He's a great sport about acting, really. Like in the attic scene of *THTDBOA*, Tommy had no problem lying face down in a pool of blood on a dirty rat-shit-encrusted floor for a long, sweaty time while we shot that scene. And when we told him to play dead, he literally turned into a cold, grey corpse in front of our eyes. No breath, no movement. He just shut his entire body down until we were finished.

One of my favorite things in *THTDBOA* is Tommy's stellar torch handling, which seems perfectly Wiseau-ian. Can you describe the things that you saw that only he could have brought to the film?
There were so many times while shooting that the crew and I had to pick our jaws up off the floor, because he over-delivered and surprised us almost every time. A good example is in the scene when Alex returns to find the landlord's office empty. We shot a few takes of that, but Tommy just didn't feel like he nailed it. He begged me for one last take, and then he did that thing where he says, "Maybe something strange is going on," and grabs his temples in anguish, and it looks so ridiculous, but it's so goddamn perfect.

It was such a joy to write a scene that could've been kind of creepy on paper, but then I'd let Tommy interpret it however he'd like. Sending him up a dark staircase with a flashlight seems like such a simple thing, script-wise, but then when he actually performs it, he's swinging the light around in a completely ineffectual manner, tromping up the steps like Frankenstein's monster, and just doing things like most normal humans don't do.

Elsewhere, Tommy delivers a lot of the intentional humor in the film excellently, and often at his own expense. What's his sense of humor like?
It's odd, to say the least. Like, he doesn't understand the anatomy of a joke, or most of the basics of storytelling, but he somehow manages to be one of the most interesting and entertaining presences I've ever witnessed. I've never once had a discussion with Tommy about why something will be funny. He just accepts what's written as gospel, and then does his absolute best to give his director what they want.

During *The Tommy Wi-Show,* I tended to write dialogue tailored to his specific voice and signature speech patterns, and I think at times I may have overdone it. Like, one time, I had written a line for Tommy to address a girl with something like, "Excuse me, person, but I do not know you." And Tommy pulled me to the side and said, "I would not call her 'person,' because that is not how you talk to a lady. Could I just call her 'girl person' instead?" I couldn't argue with that.

Another time, I had written a line for Alien to tell Tommy about how they mate with "multiple replicant wives" on their planet, and Tommy pulled me aside and told me that he didn't agree with me about this, because "that isn't how aliens have sex with each other." Not sure how he knows that, but now we all do, I suppose.

It's quite rare for Tommy to work with someone more than once, so I guess the good experience must have gone two ways . . .
I think Tommy had a blast, and for some reason, he says that he and I are "always on same page." We keep in touch, and he wanted me to help produce another pilot that he wrote, but I haven't had time in my schedule to take that on. I think he just has a hard time finding people to genuinely collaborate with, because of his demeanor and reputation. Some people just want to dress him up in dumb outfits and exploit him, but I'm more interested in pulling weirdness out of Tommy, but not having that be the only joke. I say this with total sincerity, that there is a vast, untapped mine of brilliance in Tommy Wiseau's brain, but it's going to take some special and very patient people to bring that out into the world. He's expressed frustration to me as our friendship has grown, and I know that he's been burned by certain people in the past. I won't name any names, but I totally could.

Would you like to work with him again? And what dream projects do you have in mind?
Oh God, I would work with Tommy every day. He's just a hard sell to traditional media outlets, I think. Even alternative places like Adult Swim feel kinda iffy about signing on to a project with him. I would totally agree that when Tommy assumes the role of a director or producer, you're in for a wild ride. But if Tommy is being directed by someone who can properly harness his energy, there's a lot of gold in there. I'd gladly revisit *Untold Tales* or *The Tommy Wi-Show* if I could. I have many other ideas I'd like to shoot with him, but I just haven't found the time and money to pull those off. Tommy as a Van Helsing–like monster hunter, Tommy as a kindergarten teacher . . . you name it, I've had a fantasy about it.

Tommy Explains It All (Berry, 2011)

Wiseau's rise to fame has undoubtedly been aided by the Internet, and interest in the enigmatic one has grown further through uploads of videos of him including interviews, early acting footage, and even appearances in promos for companies including Urban Outfitters.[6] The combination of his ever-growing online fan base and an unfortunate lack of risk-taking producers in film and television has seen the natural response of Tommy's popularity being honed directly to his demographic, and in 2011 this saw him feature in the release of two web series.

The first, *Tommy Explains It All,* is comprised of ten episodes of direct-to-camera interviews on a wide range of subjects, including love, acting, success and his favorite film, *Citizen Kane.* The episodes were shot by Ian Berry over two sessions, in March and May of 2011, with Berry having hosted Wiseau's appearances alongside screenings of *The Room* at Cinema 21 in Portland. The short monologues he captured in *Tommy Explains It All* form one of the most fascinating glimpses into a colorful and fascinating psyche.

Interview: Ian Berry, Director of *Tommy Explains It All*

How did *Tommy Explains It All* come about?

After Tommy's initial visit to Portland, it was quite clear he and I had a very good rapport, and in hanging around him, I discovered many things about his life and the way he thought about things that made me curious for more. So I came up with the idea to interview him about very specific topics that I thought would be mutually interesting.

The subjects you interview Tommy about really cut to the core of a lot of the things people find fascinating about him. Did it take long to think up the topics, or was it more spontaneous?

Honestly, most of the questions came pretty quickly. I thought up a handful or so, and then I simply asked my friends what they would ask of him. I made the list before and revised it slightly while filming, depending on how Tommy responded. In the end, I think there were about fifteen questions for our first session. I knew there were certain issues he would flatly not discuss, like his country of origin, his age, etc. So I just stayed away from those issues and hoped he might accidentally drop a clue or two along the way, which he actually did. For instance, in the *Citizen Kane* episode, he clearly slips and begins to talk about his childhood in Europe, at which point he catches himself and tries to correct it. Mostly, though, I wanted to give him a chance to speak at length about a great many things on which, I suspected, he had strong opinions, but had never been directly asked to address before.

Tommy's mood seems to vary throughout the videos quite substantially. How aware of that were you, in terms of what you asked? Did you have to leave anything out?

I wasn't exactly sure, of course, what topics he would have fun with and which topics would make him recoil. I had hoped he would enjoy himself, at least. I honestly planned to just ask him questions and see where it went from there.

There turned out to be a ton of footage I left on the floor. Entire subjects that just didn't work out. As I said, I went in with about fifteen questions, and I figured if half of those weren't completely garbage, I would be a very lucky man indeed.

There was one question he refused to answer altogether. I asked him what he thought about the parable of the Good Samaritan in the Bible, and he completely stonewalled me. He shut down and didn't answer the question. Once the cameras were off, he explained he didn't like to discuss religion on the record for fear of offending anyone, which I understand.

A recurring question that always yields fascinating answers: what's it like to direct Tommy Wiseau?

Directing Tommy is a very odd experience. In making the *Tommy Explains It All* videos, I didn't really direct him. I didn't want to! I had seen some of the videos other people had made with Tommy, and I felt, since I had spent some time around him, that he was so much more funny and interesting and charming and lovable when he wasn't "acting." And I felt that the people who were using him in these videos were merely exploiting him as a curiosity to be mocked, rather than giving him a chance to entertain people as the naturally charismatic and intriguing person he is. Tommy is an astoundingly gifted entertainer, but not a terribly strong actor, per se. Therefore, my real job was to get him to feel comfortable enough to just be himself. That is when, I felt, he would be his most valuable. I still feel that way.

The hardest part with regards to making the videos is that Tommy can speak at great length about almost anything and still not answer your question. He would sometimes talk for twenty minutes and eventually not remember what the question was, or where he was going with his answer. Basically, if I wasn't satisfied with his responses, I would simply rephrase the question and watch him go off for another twenty minutes in the complete opposite direction! I think you can see his very scattered and circular patterns of thought quite well in the finished videos. I didn't poke or prod too much; I just kept a very persistent attitude until he gave me enough options to work with. The challenge wasn't so much working with Tommy in person, so to speak, but rather trying to shape his answers into some sort of coherency in the editing process. That and trying to get him to speak about anything not related, in his mind, to *The Room*.

I actually wrote a feature-length screenplay for Tommy about a professional thief who had just robbed a bank. While he's hiding out in his safe house, he meets and becomes involved with his neighbors, a dysfunctional married couple who turn out to be more ruthless and cunning than him. Intended only as a demo, Tommy and I filmed the first scene of the movie, entitled *Rico the Destructor,* on his second trip to Portland for an appearance at Cinema 21—the same visit that I filmed the color episodes of *Tommy Explains It All.* Directing him for this was absolutely wonderful. It was just the two of us, and he didn't have any dialogue, so I think he felt very comfortable and free to be himself. There was no pressure to impress, no risk of failure and/or embarrassment. It was more like playing around than anything else.

Tommy Explains It All is a really great series—any chance we'll see more in the future?
I would love to continue making *Tommy Explains It All,* but it's completely and obviously dependent on if Tommy wants to do it. Personally, I don't think he ever understood why I wanted to make the videos, or why I asked him the questions I did. I don't think he ever "got it." Frankly, I don't believe Tommy understands what makes him so funny to other people. He knows other people consider him to be funny, but he just doesn't grasp what that particular brand of humor is. The last time we saw each other, he was quite warm and responsive to my ideas. So, who knows? Maybe there will be more episodes after all!

The Tommy Wi-Show (Benz, 2011)

During the editing of *The House that Drips Blood on Alex,* Brock LaBorde received a phone call from Wiseau stating that "he wanted to do a talk show . . . like a real one where he'd do a monologue, sit behind a desk, and interview celebrities." Following a series of unsuccessful pitches of this premise to various networks, a fortuitous meeting with the website Machinima.com found that there was a lust for any online content on a video game theme starring Wiseau, which LaBorde combined with the chat show element.

The Tommy Wi-Show consists of ten episodes in which see Wiseau playing a version of himself who is beamed up onto a spaceship by "Alien," who challenges him to prove his worth as Earth's ultimate video-game warrior in a series of popular titles including *Mortal Kombat, Little Big Planet 2,* and a game set in a location close to TW's heart: *Driver: San Francisco.* The show features by far Wiseau's most entertaining turn outside of *The Room* and is tonally and technically pitch-perfect, capturing both his natural and performance talents at their unique best.

Interview: Payman Benz, Director of *The Tommy Wi-Show*

In terms of the look and feel of the show, there's a resemblance to *Mystery Science Theater 3000.* What were some of the influences on the show?
We talked about *MST3K,* but beyond that, the show is pretty straightforward. We could have just had Tommy in an empty room doing the same thing and it would have still been hilarious, but it was fun to give it a weird look. Our production designer, Greg Aronowitz, is a bit of a legend, and he built the amazing set for us. Once I told him it was a Tommy Wiseau project, Greg was on board as quickly as I was.

Tommy is seemingly pretty bad at games—the *Driver* bridge segment is excruciating! Is everything we see in the show 100 percent genuine?
The game playing is 100 percent real. We didn't let Tommy even know what game he was playing until we rolled cameras and handed him the controller. The more accustomed he was to the game, the more natural comedy we'd lose. Brock also played Alien in the series, and was off-camera taunting Tommy to keep him reacting.

Some of the best parts of the show are the small jokes and things you get Tommy to say at the end of the show, like, "I'm in your base killing your dudes." I wondered, was he game for this kind of humor?

Tommy had absolutely no idea what any of these lines meant. Explaining them to him would have only caused more confusion, so we just told him that they were popular Internet phrases, and he just repeated what we told him to say.

How did Tommy respond to you as a director?

First of all, we shot for maybe four or five days total over the span of a few months, and Tommy never learned my name. He just referred to me as "Mr. Director." He was cordial to me, at best. I think in his eyes, Tommy sees himself as a director, so he has a lot of trouble letting anyone else call the shots. He'd make condescending comments, or would roll his eyes at me, but I'd ignore it because there's no way to reason with Tommy. You just roll with it, because any type of confrontation would throw off the chance of him getting his lines right. Directing him was a challenge, to say the least. He couldn't remember lines, so we resorted to shooting about 90 percent of the series line-by-line. Here's an example of what happened several times:

> **ME:** All right Tommy, you ready?
>
> **TOMMY:** Yeah, of course I'm ready. What do you think? Ha ha.
>
> **ME:** Great. And . . . action.
>
> **TOMMY:** . . . Line!
>
> **ME:** The line is, "Alien, why are you doing this to me?"
>
> **TOMMY:** OK! OK! I got it. I know, OK?
>
> **ME:** And . . . Action.
>
> **TOMMY:** . . . Line!
>
> **ME:** Alien, why are you doing this to me? . . . Action.
>
> **TOMMY:** . . . Why are you Alien . . . line!
>
> **ME:** Alien, why are you doing this to me?
>
> **TOMMY:** OK! I got it. OK, Mr. Director? Geez.
>
> **ME:** OK, great. We're still rolling, and action.
>
> **TOMMY:** . . . Line![7]

This happened many, many, many times. We'd go through this for the majority of the lines, then sometimes Tommy would randomly just steamroll through the entire scene without getting a single line wrong. It amazed and confused us every single time.

There was one moment where Tommy was yelling at Alien, who was still offscreen. And then Tommy said, "You're driving me crazy, you know that?? You are tearing …" and he stopped. We were SO excited, and then he let us down. If he would have said "You are tearing me apart, Alien!" we would have probably thrown a parade out of sheer joy, because that alone would have gotten us a couple hundred-thousand views.

One other funny thing happened on set. We moved the set to Greg Aronowitz's house for an episode, and Tommy asked me where the bathroom was. I told him to go through the kitchen, where Greg's two dogs were hanging out. Tommy walks into the kitchen, and I heard him say, "Oh, hi, doggies." He said it without a shred of irony, and was not saying it to make anyone laugh. It was one of the best moments of my life.

Future Projects

Since 2011, aside from his promotion of *The Room* and the mooted reboot of *The Neighbors,* there have been only clues and long-running hints about what Wiseau's next project could be. Outside of the unexpected release of an underwear range in November 2013, which has been sold at screenings and directly though his own store, little has been seen of his work. So, what could the future hold for Wiseau?

Since the release of *The Room,* Wiseau has often spoken about writing a book about the differences between 35 mm and HD film,[8] and as of 2014, he still claims to be in the process of completing it.[9] After eleven years, it's perhaps indicative of the possible use of such a book that no one has beaten Wiseau to the punch, which may lead some people to believe that the book is merely an attempt to disguise the unnecessary expenditure on two sets of equipment. Although he has claimed that this research provided the methodology for filming *The Room* on both, Wiseau stated in an early interview for the DVD release that the real reason was because he "was confused about these two formats." (The interview has been replaced for the Blu-ray release.)

As well as the long-rumored 3D version of *The Room,* there are two other frequently mentioned feature-film projects seemingly in production at Wiseau-Films. The first, entitled *Foreclosure,* sounds as though it may be linked thematically to *Homeless in America;* Wiseau has helpfully stated that it "relates to homes and foreclosures."[10] On a completely different note, the second concerns a thematic constant throughout Wiseau's life and career, as noted in numerous interviews and articles: vampires.[11] The as-yet-untitled "Vampire Film" has been announced as following *Foreclosure,* with Wiseau promising that it is so frightening "that you will probably not sleep for two weeks."[12] It is not yet clear whether any of these projects will actually come to fruition, with the example of *The Neighbors* sitcom making it seem as though, without significant financial backing and professional support to steer the project, Wiseau may remain in perpetual production on these and his other projects, which would be a sad loss.

27
GREG SESTERO
THE DISASTER ARTIST AND BEYOND

Outside of Wiseau's own efforts to extend the lifespan of *The Room,* its tenth anniversary was marked by the significant release, on October 1, 2013, of a book written by Greg Sestero and Tom Bissell, entitled *The Disaster Artist: My Life Inside The Room, the Greatest Bad Movie Ever Made.* After a decade of growing cult success and the development of many theories about the film's background, it was inevitable that a book revealing details of its mysterious conception would hold interest for avid fans. To a wider, uninitiated audience, it might not have seemed such a thrilling prospect, as for all intents and purposes, what the book promised was a detailed account of a niche film, written by a male-model/actor. Yet the book would quickly become a critically acclaimed, bestselling modern literary classic.

The Disaster Artist is Sestero's memoir, detailing the history of his friendship with Tommy Wiseau and their experiences of making *The Room* together. Sestero not only appears as Mark in the film but also served as line producer, fulfilling extensive and varying duties as Wiseau's right-hand man. Of anyone involved in the making of the film, Sestero was by far and away the best placed to deliver a book on the subject. The fortuitous meeting of the two lonesome, searching souls in an acting class in 1998 resulted in a friendship strengthened by a shared ambition to make it as actors. After meeting Wiseau, Sestero developed a fascination and admiration for the fearlessness of this unique and bizarre man who was seemingly blessed with a total lack of inhibition, at odds with Sestero's own lack of confidence. Their friendship eventually led to Sestero's deep involvement in the production of Wiseau's vision, *The Room.*

Sestero co-authored the book with Tom Bissell, with each writing separate drafts and combining the elements, the fusion of his unique source material and insight with steering from Bissell's literary talents resulted in an extremely tight and well-constructed read. Bissell himself is no slouch when it comes to *The Room,* having previously written one of the defining articles on the film for *Harper's,* entitled "Cinema crudité: The mysterious appeal of the post-camp cult film," in which he professes to having seen the film "at least twenty times."[1] The book benefits from the collaboration between its authors, as Sestero's emotions are astutely communicated throughout and are often deeply affecting. The intense and dysfunctional relationship between Sestero and Wiseau is reminiscent of that of Sal Paradise and Dean Moriarty in Jack Kerouac's *On the Road,* with the comparison reflected further in the deftness of the prose. In one memorable description of Wiseau's staggering early confidence as an actor, they write, "The rest of us were toying with chemistry sets and he was lighting the lab on fire."[2]

The book neatly uses "cross-cutting" throughout, as alternating scenes from Sestero's promising early career as a model and actor develop an ascending parallel relationship with the on-set chronology of the production of *The Room.* Each chapter's beginning is marked by a prophetic quote from either *The Talented Mr. Ripley* or *Sunset Boulevard,* which heightens the dramatic tension and also underlines the timelessness of the tale. The tightly constructed revelations and cliffhangers afforded by the alternating chapter structure make for a gripping read. My own initial perception of the book was to draw comparisons between it and the contemporary, adjacent hysteria surrounding the final series of the television series *Breaking Bad,* which was airing at the same time. The two share a story full of mystery, suspense, surreal weirdness, and laugh-out-loud humor that you just *have* to talk to somebody about as you go along—and yet it wouldn't be possible to bear the burden of spoiling any of these things for somebody who hasn't yet started upon the journey of the narrative.

The Disaster Artist is, at heart, a brave undertaking. It's clear that the book would not have worked had Sestero not made the decision to lay bare his own experiences, and it is this frankness that makes it so astonishing. Tommy Wiseau has been an enigmatic figure since he first came to the world's attention. His background, origins, and the financial situation allowing for the production of a completely independent $6-million film had, until now, been almost entirely mysterious, with any theories about him merely the subject of myth, rumor, and guesswork. Having known Wiseau for a number of years, Sestero is able to piece together key information about him: his humble beginnings in Europe to the dark and somewhat tragic circumstances that brought him to America; his determination in business and fondness for the American dream; the building of his Street Fashions USA retail empire, which afforded him the financial conditions necessary to make *The Room.*

The more remarkable part of this element of the book is the line drawn by the authors so as not as to fully reveal the extent of such personal information. The fact that the details of Wiseau's age, country of origin, and even his real name are things the authors probably know but do not fully divulge—despite their being the most hotly debated of subjects— shows an admirable restraint and respect for his privacy. Instead, a portrait is painted that gives the reader just enough necessary detail to begin to understand his personality. (Though the exact details are not revealed, we know, for example, that Wiseau is older than he says he is.)

The mysterious and seemingly insecure character drawn in the book is one that is in line with the person seen avoiding questions about his past at audience Q&A sessions; a man who needs privacy, be it to evade former trauma, or simply to discard any links to his past in his attempts to build a new persona as an all-American movie star.

An essential part of the wider appeal of *The Disaster Artist* is that it is a story that most of us can relate to: an intense relationship that gradually turned from something special into something unhealthy, followed by the difficulties of how to proceed beyond the breaking point. In exploring the details of that friendship, it's a credit to Sestero's own patience and loyalty that, in the intervening years, he has continued to support Wiseau, promoting *The Room* through personal appearances at screenings and press interviews, and assisting in the production of materials for the home releases of the film. Fans sometimes mistakenly take Sestero's appearances at *Room* screenings to be nonchalant or aloof, which is a misinterpretation of a laidback, thoughtful, and reflective personality, assimilating, collecting, and cataloguing his strange experiences (all to the eventual benefit of the book). Perhaps Mark's assertion in *The Room* that he's "just sitting up here thinking, you know?" is something Sestero himself can relate to.

What surely nobody can relate to is the stranger-than-fiction quality of Wiseau. The tales woven throughout *The Disaster Artist* are frankly hilarious, and so frequent, that almost every page contains something jaw-droppingly embarrassing or eye-wateringly funny. It is made clear that he is a man of grand ambition and a man of an even more grand delusion whose erratic behavior defies conventional human logic. Yet Sestero's understanding, empathy, and compassion brings a weight to the book, and woven throughout are the remnants of an almost familial love now tainted by an underlying melancholic regret. The unexpected emotional punch delivered by *The Disaster Artist* is perhaps the book's strongest quality, and is almost certainly what has made a comedic book into something profound and truly unforgettable.

The overall tone of the book is reminiscent of the narration in Rob Reiner's *Stand by Me*. As per the bittersweet delivery by Richard Dreyfuss, Sestero's recollections deliver fond, nostalgic coming-of-age stories charting the budding friendship between outsiders, related with the undertone of a narrator now bestowed with a knowledge of his story's subjects expanding beyond the timeframe of the tale. Sestero's empathy for his friend comes through, and there's a sense of catharsis, as though *The Disaster Artist* was a necessary step for him to move forward.

The similarity to *Stand by Me* is strengthened by the notion that Wiseau himself is somewhat reminiscent of Corey Feldman's character, Teddy Duchamp. Physically scarred and emotionally damaged by earlier trauma, his tall tales and determination to conceal his past are symptomatic of an outward guarding of inner vulnerability. Sensitive about his age and looks, and leading a life seemingly dogged by bad fortune, loneliness, and an overall sense of a lack of acceptance, this portrait of Wiseau leads to a greater understanding of *The Room,* and puts an entirely different spin on the film. Though it was already obvious that the film is a deeply self-involved vanity project, revolving around the character of Johnny/Tommy, it is also, at least in part, the construction of a life desired. Upon witnessing Wiseau's glee at viewing footage from the badly staged alley scene, which was so apparently awful to all else involved, Sestero notes, "In that monitor, at least, Tommy was young and had a fun life and many, many friends."[3]

Given that the book partially or fully reveals previously unknown information about Wiseau, perhaps the most intriguing question to arise from the release of the book is how he himself feels about it. Greg Sestero has been quoted as saying that Wiseau refers to *The Disaster Artist* as "The Red Bible," and has read it multiple times.[4] It's an intriguing insight, too, to note that Wiseau has developed yet another catchphrase to deflect questions about the book: "I support him 50 percent."[5] Given his trademark lack of specificity when it comes to questions he doesn't wish to answer, it's hard to pinpoint *which* 50 percent of the book exactly he disagrees with, although Sestero's methodology for researching the parts about Wiseau's personal life and background has been outlined as coming directly from him:

> **I interviewed Tommy quite a bit about his life. He opened up little by little over the years. I felt like I shared those bits that he was comfortable sharing and pieced it together. I guess when he is ready to share the rest of those gaps, well, that's his decision.[6]**

Perhaps, then, this is merely a denial in the face of some home truths, as *The Disaster Artist* reveals that the history and production of *The Room* was far, far weirder than could have been predicted by anybody that wasn't there. The tale of *The Room* may be full of unexpected events, but it is also unexpectedly full of wisdom on many subjects, including the film industry and the sacrifices and enormous luck required to make it as an actor—luck that does not touch everyone. In the wake of the Hollywood juggernaut lay not only the misfits but also those who almost made it but for some reason didn't quite get the breaks. Instead of exploiting Wiseau, Sestero has aligned himself with him, and he arguably lays his own soul more nakedly open, for he knows what the reader comes to understand: the book is the portrait of a friendship, and of a strange, strange man who is more like the rest of us than we would like to admit.

Beyond *The Disaster Artist*

The success of *The Disaster Artist* and the growth of its popularity has resulted in an astounding number of developments in a relatively short time, with a number of them having already supported or grown out of the book. A thirty-minute documentary produced by Greg Sestero and Michael Rousselet was made to go alongside the book, and has been used to promote it at screenings of *The Room,* while also forming the basis of a short promotional trailer.[7] The film features never-before-seen behind-the-scenes footage, plus interviews with members of the cast and crew, including Juliette Danielle, Robyn Paris, and Dan Janjigian, who discuss their experiences of working on the film. Notably, the film also includes the full-length version of Tommy Wiseau's now infamous Shakespearian "Street Fashions USA" advert, which has become the Holy Grail for *Room* historians. Its appearance is as fortuitous as the finding of any relic, according to Sestero, who said, "Years ago, my mom was gonna toss it in the trash, and I stopped her and said, 'You cannot throw that away.'"[8] Sestero completed the recording of an audiobook version of *The Disaster Artist* in April 2014 for release in May of the same year, with a paperback release and international publication to follow.

The release of the book has led to a secondary tidal wave of interest in *The Room* by developing new levels of intrigue and interest for existing fans but also by opening the film to a new audience. Wider interest initially came through a high level of critical praise being bestowed upon the book, with a number of glowing high-profile reviews and awards, including the 2013 bookish.com Oscar for Best Nonfiction book. Perhaps the biggest audience-growth development came following a well observed, eloquent review of the book by the actor and artist James Franco in December 2013 for *Vice,*[9] which was followed shortly, in February 2014, by the news that Franco's own Rabbit Bandini production company had optioned the rights to turn the book into a feature film, which he will also direct.[10]

The news immediately sent the online community into a frenzy of speculation, particularly concerning potential casting choices. At the time of writing, only a small number of the key personnel of the film have been confirmed by Franco. Vince Jolivette, Seth Rogen, and Evan Goldberg are the co-producers; Ryan Moody will write the script; and Franco himself is to star in the film, with his brother Dave playing Greg Sestaro.[11] Asked what he thought of the choice at a 2014 screening of *The Room,* Wiseau replied, "That's what I say, it's a good choice!"[12] One suspects that the opportunity for James Franco to play Wiseau while taking on similar duties in producing and directing the film is something that would appeal to his method acting style, and was seemingly confirmed by producer Rogen when he teased the fact that Franco "might play Wiseau" on *The Opie and Anthony Show.*[13] Franco's acclaimed turns as James Dean in Mark Rydell's 2001 TV movie *James Dean,* and as the larger-than-life, transformative character Alien in Harmony Korine's *Spring Breakers,* both show an ability to accurately portray characters directly or indirectly based on real people. Furthermore, several of his art projects, including a role in TV's *General Hospital* and 2013's "Psycho Nacirema," have displayed a creative urge in producing art based on cinema, concerned with playing with the visual medium and exploring notions of performance and persona—something that will benefit a *Disaster Artist* adaptation greatly. Most tantalizing of all is the potential teaser statement with which Franco signed off his initial *Vice* review: "In so many ways, *Tommy c'est moi.*"[14]

It's expected that film adaptation will arrive in late 2015, and the source material, along with Franco's connection to many of the high-profile comedians who are fans of *The Room,* will surely see an exciting cast of supporting characters, should that be the route he chooses to take. With an artist like Franco, anything is possible, and with Sestero giving his full approval to the project, it will be exciting to see where the film adaptation leads. Almost certainly, though, it will lead to yet more people watching *The Room* for the first time, and a boom in the growth of its success.

28

Watching *The Room,* it's inevitable that a portion of people will instantly or eventually become Roomies, buying some or all of the merchandise, reading *The Disaster Artist,* and consuming everything Tommy Wiseau has ever been in. But where do *Room* fans go next, and does the ride have to end there? Much of *The Room's* avid following (outside of the communal experience at screenings) exists online, with its presence continually reaffirmed through satellites of the official website, including an official Facebook page and fan site, as well as a continual presence on sites like Reddit and countless YouTube videos. Having developed such a rabid fan base, the lifespan of the film has been extended by a plethora of supporting materials, and many of the film's biggest fans have gone on to make tributes to *The Room* in various creative forms.

Commentary and Podcasts: *How Did This Get Made?*

Much of the appeal of the "bad movie" craze is based around the enjoyment of humor brought to commentary on and analysis of the film. With *The Room* being one of most popular examples of this vein of film, and one that it already hilarious in itself, many prominent comedians have adopted it as the subject of their acerbic wit. In 2009, an unofficial audio commentary for the film was released by Rifftrax,[1] a company founded by Mike J. Nelson, who previously starred in *Mystery Science Theater 3000*—an original pioneer of "riffing" on bad films. Rifftrax is a platform for Nelson and other comedians to release unofficial audio downloads that the user then pairs with the relevant title (a release technique devised to circumvent legal issues). Due to the nature of such online criticism and the necessity to use the film itself in their creation, copyright issues have been raised elsewhere, with a prominent video review by the Nostalgia Critic temporarily removed at the request of Wiseau-Films,[2] although the video did return later in 2010.

A number of podcasts discussing the film have been recorded, often including interviews with the cast or Wiseau himself, owing to the ease of making use of recordings of phone interviews, or the audio from video conferencing. The use of such communication has proven a useful tool for Wiseau to promote projects, with the distance allowing him to be typically evasive, perhaps best typified by his podcast interview with *Proudly Resents,* to which he gave a particularly uncooperative interview.[4] Since its creation in 2010, Earwolf's *How Did This Get Made?* has been perhaps the most successful humorous podcast based around the concept of dissecting bad films, largely owing to the caliber of comedians and guest stars it features. Presented by Paul Scheer, June Diane Raphael, and Jason Mantzoukas, the episode concerning *The Room* (#23) was released on November 15, 2011, with guests Greg Sestero and Steve Heisler providing expert insight into the film.

Interview: Paul Scheer, Host of *How Did This Get Made?*

How did you first hear about *The Room,* and where did you first see it?
I first remember hearing about *The Room* via a billboard in Hollywood. I had just had moved to L.A., and *The Room* had a giant billboard in a prime spot on Highland, just south of Hollywood. I was always passing it. I just assumed it was some indie film about a vampire. I never researched it, I just assumed it was a horror movie, and not till friends started to talk about it, did I realize, "Oh, that's the vampire movie." When I first

saw it, I didn't know what to expect, but it was oddly exactly as my friends described—but totally different than I imagined. It was like a bizarro Tennessee Williams play.

Why do you think *The Room* has become such a phenomenal success over other bad films?
It's like the pyramids: we'll never truly understand how/why it's so perfectly constructed. It's like watching a mental patient's ballet; sure, it's not good by traditional standards, but it's brilliant because it's unlike anything you've ever seen.

How many times have you seen the film?
Probably six or seven times. Unlike other "so bad it's good" films, it's really watchable, and I find something new every time. He's a genius.

What do you love and/or hate most about *The Room*?
Hate: the sex scene. It's too intense. It's like watching a sloppy bag of muscles hump. Love: the fact that I've seen it multiple times and I still don't get all the relationships.

Have you ever been to a public screening?
I was lucky enough to see a screening in L.A. with Tommy in attendance. It's everything you want it to be. He comes out to greet the line, tosses a football around, and then does a Q&A before the film. In many ways, it's the better version of *The Rocky Horror Picture Show,* because when you see *TRHPS,* the cast doesn't show up in character—and Tommy certainly does. I will say that I think the best way to see *The Room* is to watch it first with friends and then get the theater experience. They really complement each other. But don't do it the other way around. Live screenings are too rowdy, and don't let you take in its majesty of this film in its entirety.

Lastly, how was it to have Greg Sestero on *How Did This Get Made*?
The most surprising thing about Greg is how normal he is, and while he gets the joke, he's surprisingly compassionate about Tommy. His book is a must for anyone interested in movies or life!

Video Game: *The Room Tribute*

September 2010 saw the release of what has become one of the most high-profile *Room* tributes, a video game by Newgrounds.com, fittingly titled *The Room Tribute.* A point-and-click role-playing game in which the player controls Johnny, guiding him through the events of the film, the story follows his actions throughout *The Room* and also outside of the scenes in which he doesn't appear. It's interesting to note that the narrative of *The Room* actually works much more effectively this way, and some of the limp plot revelations of the film, such as Lisa's affair with Mark, have an actual impact. The game is devilishly addictive, layered, and lovingly created, featuring dialogue from the film, an 8-bit version of the original score, beautifully observed in-jokes, and compelling gameplay. It has been extremely well received by fans, and is a highly recommended experience . . . just make sure you visit Denny's place from day one.

Interview: Tom Fulp, Creator of *The Room Tribute*

How did you first come across *The Room*?

I first heard about *The Room* in an *Entertainment Weekly* article,[4] and was curious enough to order the DVD. We watched it at the Newgrounds office and were instantly hooked. I've seen it at least ten times now. When friends from the site came by our office to visit, we would inevitably break out the DVD and have a viewing party. It was always such a good time, it never failed to entertain everyone.

At what point did you think, "Wait, we could make a game out of this?" and how did that project start?

It was maybe the fourth time we showed it at the office. We had joked a few times in the past about turning it into a game, but this time we decided to roll up our sleeves and get to work. The original plan was to have it done in one week, but we soon extended that to a month after I had transcribed the script and Jeff [Bandelin[5]] had the character art down. The final game ended up taking six solid months.

One of the great things about the game is that it's filled with in-jokes and references. Did you always know people would appreciate these, or was it more for your own amusement?

It was a combination of both. We wanted to achieve an insane level of detail to mesmerize fans, but we were also having tons of fun the entire time.

At the time of writing, *The Room Tribute* has had almost 1.8 million views. How does that feel?

It feels awesome! We were worried the whole thing might be too niche, and there might only be a few thousand fans out there who would care, but fortunately the movie keeps growing in infamy.

Have you had any response from anyone in the film about *The Room Tribute*?

To my knowledge, Tommy, Greg Sestero, Juliette Danielle, and Philip Haldiman have all seen it and like it. Greg reached out to me when he was on his book tour for *The Disaster Artist* and we got to meet up, which was just mind-blowing.

Videos and Songs: The Brooklyn Doctors and Cossbysweater

The lengthier online criticism and analysis of *The Room* is complemented by shorter, snappier videos and memes celebrating the film. Clips from the film itself are some of the most popular viral videos, with one of several YouTube clips of the evergreen flower shop scene currently at over two million views.[6] Pictures of the cast (generally Wiseau himself) with dialogue from the film form a large basis of *Room* memes, alongside crossover humor such as a mash-up of *The Dark Knight* and *The Room* with the phrase, "Wiseau Serious?" Shorter parody videos with similar humor also exist, with re-edited footage including montages, the extended looping of scenes, and a personal favorite, a digitally manipulated version of the "Lisa's neck" scene in which Tommy Wiseau himself pops out of the mysterious bulge.[7]

Some of the more creative and popular tributes to *The Room* have come in song form, and two stand above all others. In 2009, the Brooklyn Doctors released "Tommy Wiseau's *The Room* rap," which parodies the film. Featuring lines such as "Lisa's so hot and Mark's his best friend / Twenty-five sex scenes that seem like they'll never end," the song has gone on to become the band's most popular upload, with over 130,000 views. Four years later, Cossbysweater released "Leave: The Room Song," a reference-heavy song written from the perspective of Mark, released at the same time as *The Disaster Artist,* and with a video starring Greg Sestero.

Interview: Greg DeLiso and Mark Breese, The Brooklyn Doctors

Where did the idea for *"The Room* rap" come from?

MARK: We had been doing a fairly steady stream of songs for a few months beforehand, mostly just whatever dumb ideas we had at the time. The first one was called "The Couch Song," and was about how I don't like to do anything and would rather just sit home, so that was very personal and true to life, but the music video that I cut together for it incorporated a lot of footage from some of my favorite movies and TV shows, including a couple clips from *The Room.* Around that time, we were all really into watching reruns of *To Catch a Predator,* so we decided to get together and do a tribute song for that show, and even though they weren't making new episodes anymore, it still got some decent traction and went somewhat viral online. I think after that we realized that we could take things we loved and make songs about them, and hopefully catch some of the audience that way. It was really all just for fun, though, and we had no expectation that it would lead to anything necessarily. We realized that *The Room* was starting to catch fire, and that nobody at that point had made a song about it yet, so we'd be first to market. We showed the movie to our friends, Ned Martin and George Gross, who had never seen it, but they fell in love immediately. They decided to reach out to Tommy and arrange the first NYC screening of *The Room.* At that point, we decided the timing was right and went to work on it right away to coincide with the screening date.

Did you know there would be an appetite for it?

MARK: I think we felt that there would be an audience for it, but we were mostly just doing it for fun. We had done a few other videos that caught on online and thought this would be a no-brainer. I don't think we really worked all that hard on it. Peter [Litvin, third member of the Brooklyn Doctors] did the heavy lifting with the music production, which took some time, but we all got together and wrote the lyrics in basically one night, I think, and recorded it the next day, so it all came together relatively quickly.

What was the creative process? Did you all pitch in ideas for things to mock/reference?

MARK: We were so fully immersed in the movie, watching it all the time that the lyrics and all the elements we wanted to talk about were fairly obvious to us. We all got together to have a brainstorming session to come up with lyric ideas. I remember us talking about what the hook would be, and we weren't coming up with anything that great. I got up and went to the bathroom and while I was in there I came up with the line, "*The Room* is in the house," which I thought was really dumb, but I thought also had the same kind of "so bad it's good" quality that the movie does.

GREG: I was just the video guy, mostly, and I helped with lyrics. The only line I remember coming up with was, "Who the fuck cares that he shaved," which Greg Sestero later quoted to me when we met! Mark and Peter are the real musical geniuses—especially Pete, who did all of our music and recording.

The editing of the video is sublime, and it's clear that you know the film inside out. How many viewings did this kind of knowledge require?
GREG: Ha, thanks! I've probably seen it at least a dozen times. It's very mesmerizing. I love showing it to new people.
MARK: When we first discovered it, we had it running on a loop at our apartment for a couple weeks straight. Every night I would come home and Greg would point out something that he heard or saw for the first time, and we just got more and more into it over time.

Have you had any response about the rap from anyone involved with the movie?
GREG: Yeah, this is the best part! So, first we heard on MySpace that Greg Sestero was a fan, because he was posting the lyrics to it! Greg has become a good pal. He's always supported us and just been great.

The real good part, though, is meeting Tommy. Tommy must have a Google alert for his name or something, because he immediately heard about it. This was right at the time of the first screening, so he asked George Gross, "Who are these Brooklyn Doctors?" George didn't know whether Tommy was mad or not, so he denied knowing us but put us in touch. So, the day after the first ever NYC screening, we met Tommy in his hotel lobby. Again, we didn't know what to think, because the song is pretty mean, but Tommy loved it! He was very, very sweet. He gave us T-shirts. Legend has it he still has Peter's CD in his car CD platter rotation.

The meeting was very odd and classic Tommy. He loved the video and song but he didn't like that I had used low-quality footage from the movie. He said people in New York don't care about quality. He also lectured us about copyright law, for about an hour, and said that people in New York don't care about copyright like people in L.A. do.
MARK: After that he took us to a bodega-type place to eat lunch, at which point he was talking to us about how he wanted to have screenings for the movie in Central Park in front of a million people, and also at Yankee Stadium. He also said that we should perform at these shows along with the Scissor Sisters, who were also big fans. While he's telling us his big plans and gesturing wildly about them, we all noticed that the entire time he had a big piece of corn or a chickpea caught in his hair, and it

was hard for us to not bust out laughing. Overall, he was really nice to us and even paid for our lunch, although he did make me carry around his laptop for the rest of the afternoon for no reason.

The song pulls absolutely no punches. Were you concerned about the response from the cast?

GREG: We weren't concerned initially, but since then we kind of regret calling Lisa fat. We only did it because it's a thing people yell out at the screenings. We didn't mean she's actually fat. Clearly she's not.

MARK: I get why it sounds like a harsh line, and it is, but it was in line with the crowd reactions at all the screenings when Tommy is talking about her beauty and stuff. Greg Sestero didn't have a problem with any of the lyrics and oddly enough neither did Tommy. The only note Tommy really gave us other than the bizarre copyright stuff is that he didn't like the movie clip at the end, the "let's go eat, huh?" scene. He thought that didn't need to be there, but the thorough evisceration we gave him in the rest of the song, he seemed totally fine with—either that, or he didn't understand it entirely.

How has the song been received, and how does it fare against your other videos?

GREG: It's been great. When the video came out we had friends of friends telling them to check it out, people that didn't know us. It's definitely been our most successful video.

MARK: People seem to really like it, and you'll see people leave comments on it that say they put it on their iPod or that they listen to it once a month or something. So it's nice that while it's not a smash success, and we certainly didn't make a dime off of it, it connected with the audience we were aiming for. It's stuck around for over five years, and whenever new people discover the movie for the first time, they invariably end up finding our song. It's pretty cool to be a part of the extended universe of *The Room* somewhat.

Interview: Allie Goertz, Cossbysweater

When did you think about turning *The Room* into a song, and how did you approach it?

Over the summer [of 2013], I spent much of my time making YouTube videos at the YouTube Space in L.A. I was part of a group called "Geek Lab," [and we were] asked to create more content than I was used to. I wracked my brain and came up with the idea to write a song from Mark's POV. I chose Mark because he is the most human and real of *The Room* characters. Mark also has my favorite quote in the whole movie, which would become the basis of my song: "Leave your stupid comments in your pocket." I found that the song wrote itself.

How did Greg Sestero come to be in the video, and how was the shoot?
I made a quick demo of the song, and the folks at YouTube told me to get in touch with Michael Rousselet. I reached out to him and was so happy to find that he liked it. If I could impress *him,* I knew was in good hands. He told me that he and Greg Sestero are good friends, and that he could put us in touch. I sent the song to Greg and Michael put in a good word. Within no time, the Sestosterone was on board.

Stage 5 TV and I worked together to produce the track and create a dark and beautiful music video starring Greg. It wasn't until I saw him in our re-creation of the set of *The Room* that it really hit me how amazing this all was. What's best is that Greg couldn't be nicer or more fun to work with. Working with him was a delight and is something I'll always be proud of. He dealt with my insane nerves like a champ and was patient with me when I had to do our "kiss" scene a dozen times. The entire shoot was a dream, but my favorite moment is the pillow fight. My smile is completely genuine, and the happiest I've ever been on tape. If I didn't have documented proof, I'd have thought it was a dream.

Have you had any response from anyone else from the film about the song?
I actually met the entire cast, including Tommy, on Greg's book-release party at the New Beverly in L.A. It was a trip to see everyone together and know they had all seen my music video. Making a song and music video about *The Room* is one of my greatest joys and makes me feel like a contributing member to the society of *Room* fans. I hope to do a lot with my career, but I know this shoot will always be the thing I'm most proud of.

Stage Adaptations

Outside of the realm of the Internet—or "real life," as it is known—a number of theatrical projects have taken *The Room* to new heights. Wiseau himself has often talked about taking the film to Broadway as a musical adaptation,[8] although that is currently another project of his that is yet to come to light. However, in June 2011, Wiseau and Greg Sestero took part in a live reading of the original script for *The Room* at the AFI Silver in Washington, D.C., with a number of hilarious preview trailers released showing Wiseau directing rehearsals.[9] Sestero has resurrected the format himself, giving live readings from the original script as part of the *Disaster Artist* book tour.[10]

Wiseau's failure to create a finished *Room* musical of his own has seen others emerge from fans, including *The Room: The Musical* in Chicago. *You're Tearing Me Apartment: The Roomsical* was created further afield, in Australia. In March 2013, after three years in preparation, and a decade after the release of its inspiration, *The Roomsical* hit the creaky panels of a small Melbourne stage. The Melbourne International Comedy Festival seemed as good a kick-start for the show as any, but reliance on a burgeoning city of international comedy enthusiasts would not equate to a guaranteed audience. Over the next eleven nights, with wavering, largely word-of-mouth attendances, *The Roomsical* would play to more than 1,200 audience members. A few weeks later, the show's Sydney debut sold out so quickly that a second show was added, and this led to the show being picked up for another four nights later in the year during the Sydney Fringe Fest.

For now, it appears that it's back to the drawing board for *The Roomsical,* with a new version, more reliant on puppets, currently being work-shopped. Plans are afoot to take the new, improved show around the world.

Interview: Matt Downey, Creator of *The Roomsical*

What inspired you to write and make *The Roomsical*?
Three things: the majesty of the train wreck film itself, a new electric piano that was screaming for attention, and a visit to *Jersey Boys,* a musical about Frankie Valli. I was dragged kicking and screaming to the theater, but after an hour and a half of group clapping and schlocky dialogue to justify a few songs, I was turned around completely and itching to get home to the keyboard.

Tommy Wiseau has been talking about taking *The Room* to Broadway. Did this have any influence on your own project, or cause you any concern?
It's pretty much the opening line in our show. There have been versions of the show where we have replicated the extra features interview with Tommy where he states just that.

How did you go about filling such big shoes when casting?
It's a tough one, and the reason we haven't left the country with it just yet. Our biggest problem is how often the cast needs to double up and play another recognizable personality. Our Tommy, for example, plays a number of characters, including Chris-R, so that's two lots of big shoes to fill. It's a heavy expectation on any actor's range. It's why we've currently taken it back to the drawing board and are now considering masks or puppets. It would mean being able to cast actors regardless of physical stature, height, ethnicity, etc.

Tell me about the life of *The Roomsical,* and the reactions you've received to it.
I'd say that overall it's been well received, and I've seldom answered to any significant criticism, but comedy festival crowds are odd. Die-hards would bring spoons and taunt the performers, but there was always a contingent of the audience who had never seen the film, and *The Roomsical* is a departure—or poetic license—enough from the movie for newcomers anyway. The few people who'd just ventured out to see a new musical with their AAA comedy passes always looked more violated than perplexed.

How many people came to see your show that haven't seen the film? Have you turned a lot of people onto the movie?
Later in our appearances, word had spread enough for the audiences to be 90 percent *Room*antics—that's what I refer to us as. It would be difficult to say how many people sought out the film as a result of our show, but I know my enthusiasm for people to see it has meant a few hundred dollars in the pocket of Wiseau-Films. The cast and their families to name but a few. *"See mum, this is why I sing lots of songs about getting fucked."*

Have you had any response from anyone involved with *The Room*?
Juliette Danielle posed with a *Roomsical* T-shirt and posted it on Facebook. She was very supportive during its initial run. Greg Sestero is aware, because he's been accosted twice by a fan in the States wearing a *Roomsical* tee, and he inquired about it both times. Greg Ellery also wished us well and asked us to let him know where he could see it, stating that our portrayal of him couldn't be any worse than the original.

EPILOGUE: THE FUTURE OF *THE ROOM*

It has been the objective of this book to try to capture some of the motivations and techniques that have seen an independently made film grow from one man's vision to an internationally beloved success: the intangible qualities of the film that make it seemingly endlessly watchable and fascinating; the mysterious qualities of Tommy Wiseau; the communal expression and celebration at screenings; a viral culture of sharing and inflicting the film on others; a host of influential early adopters; clever marketing and reinvention; the obsessive adoption of the film into other forms; and, above all, the continual reassurance of its presence. Be it a billboard advertisement in L.A., relentless touring and online promotion, or mere word of mouth as fans discover the film and take it upon themselves to keep it going, *The Room* has never faded away.

These are just part of an incredible list of elements that have come together to create the success of a film that continues to be screened on a regular basis to ever-increasing audiences, eleven years following its initial release. The serendipitous fortune of these combined variables may form a large part of explaining the success of a film which under different circumstances could have disappeared without a trace, although one suspects that even if you were to meticulously replicate these in an attempt to follow in *The Room's* footsteps, it would undoubtedly end in failure. Like its creator, then, the film is most likely a one-off happening.

At the time of writing, it seems as though there are no signs of a slowing down in the growth of *The Room* phenomenon, with screenings across the world still selling out in 2014, including at the Prince Charles Cinema in London, which held multiple sold-out screenings in February, with up to three sell-out shows in one evening alone. Continuing sales of *The Disaster Artist* and the prospect of James Franco's mooted feature film in 2015 should see the growth of a wider audience, with the appetites of fanatics fed by the fan projects of the last chapter, which show no sign of stopping. Other upcoming projects include a feature-length documentary about the film by director Rick Harper entitled *Room Full of Spoons,* scheduled for release in late 2014.

Though it may be evident that ingredients from other successful cult films—like the audience participation of *The Rocky Horror Picture Show,* or the "so bad it's good" film and backstory combination of *Troll 2* and

Best Worst Movie—are in place, Wiseau's creation transcends these by encompassing both and still having several more strings to its proverbial bow. Yet it seems to be largely agreed that despite the clever marketing, extended works, and sense of fun surrounding *The Room,* the greatest appeal is still the film itself—and, of course, Tommy Wiseau. As the figurehead and guardian of its legacy, and with his relentless optimism and sense of pride toward his creation, it seems likely that *The Room's* doors will continue to be open for as long as he is still on the planet, and even more cinemagoers will walk in and find themselves welcomed by a warm, "Oh hai!"

NOTES

Introduction: The *Room* Phenomenon

1   Feirstein, B. Original screenplay for *Tomorrow Never Dies* (Spottiswoode, 1997)
2   IMDb review, "This film is like getting stabbed in the head," by RCarstairs, June 28, 2003, accessed on March 2 2014, www.imdb.com/user/ur2424961/.
3   Medved, Harry, and Randy Dreyfuss. *The Fifty Worst Films of All Time (And How They Got That Way)*. Warner Books, 1978.
4   Red Letter Media—Star Wars Episode I: The Phantom Menace, accessed on May 14, 2014, http://redlettermedia.com/plinkett/star-wars/star-wars-episode-1-the-phantom-menace/.
5   "Interview with Tommy Wiseau" from *The Room,* directed by Tommy Wiseau (Wiseau-Films, 2003), DVD.
6   "Episode 6: What is Comedy?" *Tommy Explains it All* (Berry, 2010), accessed on March 14, 2013, www.youtube.com/watch?v=zFtwyrc-lhA.
7   Casciato, C. "Tommy Wiseau on the legacy of *The Room,*" August 8, 2013, accessed on March 17, 2014, http://blogs.westword.com/showandtell/2013/08/tommy_wiseau_on_the_legacy_of.php.
8   The film is best bought direct from the Official *Room* store at www.theroommovie.com/buydirect.html

2. How to Throw a Spoon: The Viewer's Guide

1   Promotional quote from Wiseau-Films to promote screenings, as sent via e-mail on September 13, 2013.
2   Said literally hundreds of times at screenings worldwide and quoted on *The Room* Denmark official page, accessed on February 20, 2014, www.theroommovie.com/denmark.html.
3   Interview with author, April 3, 2014.
4   Interview with author, April 6, 2014.
5   Interview with author, March 30, 2014.
6   Sestero, Greg, *The Disaster Artist* (Simon & Schuster, 2013), p.127.
7   "CNN Interview—'The Room,'" uploaded August 16 2011, accessed April 13, 2014, www.youtube.com/watch?v=kEfJ4jEH69A
8   "*The Room:* Director's edition," episode 23 of *How Did This Get Made?,* November 15, 2011, www.earwolf.com/episode/the-room-directors-edition/
9   "Tommy Wiseau Interview Part 2," uploaded April 14, 2011, accessed on February 13, 2014, www.youtube.com/watch?v=2EjDCkPALOs

10 "Tommy Wiseau Gets Hit by Football," uploaded on January 9, 2011, accessed on February 23, 2014, www.youtube.com/watch?v=siQ8zTCEOc4.

11 "Bristol Bad Film Club's Question to Tommy Wiseau and Greg Sestero at the Prince Charles Cinema," uploaded on February 10, 2014, accessed on February 24, 2014, www.youtube.com/watch?v=3JyjPiSVF1w.

12 "Tommy Wiseau recites a sonnet," uploaded on March 21, 2009, accessed on March 14, 2014, www.youtube.com/watch?v=-76HUrNa15Q.

13 Now publically revealed to be Wiseau himself by Sestero, G. *The Disaster Artist* p8.

14 Interview with author, March 12, 2014.

15 Interview with author, March 17, 2014.

16 Received Oct 9 2013.

17 Interview with author, March 30, 2014.

3. How to Create a Cult Phenomenon

1 Collis, C. "The Crazy Cult of 'The Room,'" *Entertainment Weekly,* December 12, 2008, accessed February 10, 2014, www.ew.com/ew/article/0,,20246031,00.html.

4. How to Infect Others with the *Room* Virus

1 Rose, S. "Is this the worst movie ever made?" *The Guardian,* September 10, 2009, accessed February 16, 2014, www.theguardian.com/film/filmblog/2009/sep/10/cinema-the-room-cult.

Part Two

7. 10x10, Part One

1 United States Census Bureau, accessed on March 14, 2014, www.census.gov/census2000/states/us.html.

9. 10x10, Part Two

1 *AFI Life Achievement Award: A Tribute to George Lucas* (Horvitz, 2005)

10. Denny: Philip Haldiman Interview

1 *My Big Break* is available from www.philiphaldiman.com/

11. 10x10, Part Three

1 Collins, C. "Extreme Method Acting," December 16 2013, accessed on January 10, 2014, http://entertainment.ie.msn.com/celebrity/extreme-method-acting-3?page=13.

12. The Flower Shop Scene

1 "Tommy Wiseau & Greg Sestero (THE ROOM) LIVE with Beth and Videogum," uploaded August 3 2013, accessed on February 17, 2014, www.youtube.com/watch?v=e6RtfG7D5dY.

2 Interview with the author, April 10, 2014.

3   Sestero, G. *The Disaster Artist,* p256.
4   Ibid.

14. Chris-R: Dan Janjigian Interview
1   Sestero, G. *The Disaster Artist,* p34.
2   Ibid. p98.
3   Collis, C. "The Crazy Cult of *The Room.*"

15. 10x10, Part Five
1   Sestero, G. *The Disaster Artist,* p26.

16. Michelle: Robyn Paris Interview
1   Birns & Sawyer is the LA camera-rental house from which Tommy Wiseau purchased equipment and hired crew for *The Room,* and is also where the sets for the principle shoot were built.

18. Peter: Kyle Vogt Interview
1   Sestero, G. *The Disaster Artist,* p62.

19. 10x10, Part Seven
1   Yoshimoto, M. *Kurosawa: Film Studies and Japanese Cinema* (Duke University Press, 2000), p191.

20. The Music of *The Room*
1   "'The Room'—THE ORIGINAL OPENING TITLES THEME," uploaded October 29 2013, accessed on April 22, 2014, www.youtube.com/watch?v=iS4QJImQnfo.

24. Citizen Johnny: Welles vs. Wiseau
1   Collis, C. "The Crazy Cult of *The Room.*"
2   Mulvey, L. "Citizen Kane," p453. *BFI Film Classics, Vol 1.* Edited by White, R. and Buscombe, E. (Fitzroy Dearborn, 2003).
3   Collis, C. "The Crazy Cult of *The Room.*"
4   Ebert, R. "A Viewer's Companion to *Citizen Kane,*" accessed on April 14, 2014, www.rogerebert.com/rogers-journal/a-viewers-companion-to-citizen-kane.
5   In many places, but best of all in episode 1, of *Tommy Explains It All,* accessed on February 10, 2014, www.youtube.com/watch?v=3XtsF104BZQ.
6   Ibid.

25. 10x10, Part Ten
1   Truffaut, F. *Hitchcock* (Secker & Warburg, 1968).
2   Dyer, G. *Zona: A Book about a Film about a Journey to a Room* (Canongate Books, 2012).

Part Three

26. The Further Works of Tommy Wiseau

1 Mentioned in Collis, C. "The Crazy Cult of '*The Room*,'" Sestero, G. *The Disaster Artist,* p57, and episode 1 of *Tommy Explains it All,* accessed on May 10, 2014, www.youtube.com/watch?v=3XtsF104BZQ to name a few.

2 *The Neigbors* official site, accessed on March 15, 2014, www.theneighborssitcom.com.

3 The official YouTube channel, accessed on February 20, 2014, www.youtube.com/user/TheWiseauFilms.

4 The release date was October 1, 2013.

5 Kong now says the project is unlikely to wrap in May.

6 "Tommy Wiseau's *The Neighbors* Trailer," uploaded January 13, 2009, accessed February 15, 2014, www.youtube.com/watch?v=YGpwxHMUndk.

7 *Playboy Adventures,* "Episode 2," uploaded May 28, 2006, accessed on March 1, 2014, www.channel101.com/episode/384.

8 Editor's Note: There's a moment in which Alex sucks some of the dripping blood from his finger and exclaims, "This tastes familiar," which could be read as a play on Wiseau's vampire persona.

9 Something Wiseau also pitched during *The Room* according to G. Sestero, *The Disaster Artist* p92.

10 "Tommy Wiseau Wishes YOU A Happy Memorial Day!" May 23 2013, accessed on February 10 2014, www.youtube.com/watch?v=R799vrY6zVA.

11 This mirrors Greg Sestero's description of Wiseau on the set of *The Room* in *The Disaster Artist,* p128.

12 www.theroommovie.com/buydirect.html.

13 Heisler, S. "Tommy Wiseau," June 24, 2009, accessed on March 10, 2014, www.avclub.com/article/tommy-wiseau-29598.

14 Orlikoff, D. "Wiseau is in 'The Room,'" accessed on May 2, 2014, www.columbiachronicle.com/arts_and_culture/article_b7c65dbd-8a19-5ebc-97a9-242572a96964.html?mode=jqm.

15 "Tommy Wiseau announces his next film, *Foreclosure*" uploaded on June 15, 2012, accessed on April 20, 2014, www.youtube.com/watch?v=iC4O4ERRGTU.

16 O'Neal, S. "Tommy Wiseau Planning *The Room* 3-D," December 21 2010, accessed on March 11, 2014, www.avclub.com/article/tommy-wiseau-planning-ithe-room-3-d-i-49344.

17 See the hilarious "Vampire Trick" story from Sestero, G. *The Disaster Artist,* p84.

18 Knegt, P. "The Room" Director Tommy Wiseau Says a Sitcom and a Vampire Movie are Next: The Interview, Part 2," June 10 2011, accessed on March 10 2014, www.indiewire.com/article/tommy_wiseau_part_2.

27. Greg Sestero, *The Disaster Artist* and Beyond

1 Bissell, T. "Cinema crudité: The mysterious appeal of the post-camp cult film." *Harper's,* August 2010.

2 Sestero, G. *The Disaster Artist,* p45.

3 Sestero, G. *The Disaster Artist,* p45.

4 "Greg Sestero AMA: The Sequel," February 23, 2014, accessed on February 25, 2014, www.reddit.com/r/IAmA/comments/1ynfhz/hi_reddit_its_greg_sestero_mark_from_the_room/.

5 Boyle, N. "Interview: Tommy Wiseau and Greg Sestero of The Room," March 10 2014, accessed on April 1, 2014, http://film.list.co.uk/article/58930-interview-tommy-wiseau-and-greg-sestero-of-the-room/.

6 Bacher, D. "Remembering 'The Room': Actor Greg Sestero on the cult film's ten-year anniversary," October 4, 2013, accessed on February 10, 2014, www.rollingstone.com/movies/news/remembering-the-room-20131004.

7 "THE DISASTER ARTIST: My Life Inside THE ROOM, the Greatest Bad Movie Ever Made," uploaded September 20, 2013, accessed on March 15, 2014, www.youtube.com/watch?v=Eh9lC7IBJvl.

8 "Oh Hi, Mark! An Evening with Greg Sestero: The Disaster Artist," uploaded on December 30, 2013, accessed on March 13, 2014, www.youtube.com/watch?v=e5Vl1DuKmL8#t=29.

9 Franco, J. "Universalising Art: 'The Disaster Artist' And 'The Room,'" December 5, 2013, accessed on February 10, 2014, www.vice.com/en_uk/read/universalizing-art-the-disaster-artist-and-the-room.

10 "James Franco's Production Company Acquires Book About So-Bad-It's-Good Cult Movie 'The Room,'" February 7, 2014, accessed on February 8, 2014, www.deadline.com/2014/02/james-franco-disaster-artist-movie-the-room/.

11 James Franco official Instagram page, http://instagram.com/p/kl_1EBy9ab/.

12 "James Franco Is James Franco, Yet Again," June 10, 2014, accessed on June 22, 2014, www.latimes.com/entertainment/movies/moviesnow/la-et-mn-james-franco-dave-room-lindsay-lohan-story-class-20140610-story.html.

13 "Seth Rogen talks Cult Movie, *The Room*," uploaded on May 8, 2014, accessed on May 10, 2014, www.youtube.com/watch?v=GYI6OSxpYMY.

14 Franco, J. "Universalising Art: 'The Disaster Artist' and 'The Room.'"

28. The Best of the Extended *Room*niverse

1 Rifftrax *The Room* audio commentary, June 18, 2009, www.rifftrax.com/rifftrax/room.

2 "Pissing Off a Movie Critic by Claiming Copyright Over a Video Review . . . Probably Not Smart," July 22, 2010, accessed on February 15, 2014, www.techdirt.com/articles/20100721/15284610310.shtml.

3 "The Tommy Wiseau Interview!" September 27, 2011, accessed on April 10, 2014, http://proudlyresents.com/tommyw/.

4 Collis, C. "The Crazy Cult of 'The Room.'"

5 Otherwise known as JohnnyUtah, see http://johnnyutah.newgrounds.com/.

6 "The Room—The Flower Shop Scene," uploaded June 13, 2009, accessed February 15, 2014, www.youtube.com/watch?v=7S9Ew3TIeVQ.

7 "The Room Neck Scene Redux," uploaded February 25, 2011, accessed April 27, 2014, www.youtube.com/watch?v=7IYUPmx4EHo.

8 As early as the release of *The Room* on Wiseau-Films DVD in December 2005, in "An Interview with Tommy Wiseau."

9 Including "How to Play a Drug Dealer (with Tommy Wiseau)," uploaded on June 11, 2011, accessed on May 1, 2014, www.youtube.com/watch?v=jrxIht0SPXc.

10 "The Room—performed live—with Greg Sestero," uploaded on November 16, 2013, accessed on April 3, 2014, www.youtube.com/watch?v=rq3yvgUeGmk.

Books

Dyer, G. *Zona: A Book about a Film about a Journey to a Room.* (Edinburgh: Canongate Books, 2012).

Medved, Harry, and Dreyfuss, R. *The Fifty Worst Films of All Time (And How They Got That Way).* (New York: Warner Books, 1978)

Mulvey, L. *Citizen Kane* from BFI Film Classics, Vol 1. Edited by White, R. and Buscombe, E. (London: Fitzroy Dearborn, 2003).

Sestero, G. *The Disaster Artist.* (New York: Simon & Schuster, 2013).

Yoshimoto, M. *Kurosawa: Film Studies and Japanese Cinema* (Durham: Duke University Press, 2000).

Truffaut, F. *Hitchcock.* (London: Secker & Warburg, 1968).

Online Resources

Articles

Bacher, D. "Remembering 'The Room': Actor Greg Sestero on the cult film's ten-year anniversary," October 4, 2013, accessed on February 10, 2014, www.rollingstone.com/movies/news/remembering-the-room-20131004.

Bookish editors, "Oscar-Style Nominations for Our Favorite Books of 2013," March 3, 2014, accessed on March 10, 2014, www.bookish.com/articles/oscar-adaptation-book-nominations.

Boyle, N. "Interview: Tommy Wiseau and Greg Sestero of The Room," March 10, 2014, accessed on April 1, 2014, http://film.list.co.uk/article/58930-interview-tommy-wiseau-and-greg-sestero-of-the-room/.

Casciato, C. "Tommy Wiseau on the legacy of *The Room*," August 8, 2013, accessed on March 17, 2014 http://blogs.westword.com/showandtell/2013/08/tommy_wiseau_on_the_legacy_of.php.

Collins, C. "Extreme Method Acting," December 16, 2013, accessed on January 10, 2014, http://entertainment.ie.msn.com/celebrity/extreme-method-acting-3?page=13.

Collis, C. "The Crazy Cult of 'The Room,'" *Entertainment Weekly,* December 12, 2008, accessed February 10, 2014, www.ew.com/ew/article/0,,20246031,00.html.

The Deadline Team, "James Franco's Production Company Acquires Book About So-Bad-It's-Good Cult Movie 'The Room,'" February 7, 2014, accessed on February 8, 2014, www.deadline.com/2014/02/james-franco-disaster-artist-movie-the-room/.

Ebert, R. "A Viewer's Companion to "Citizen Kane," accessed on April 14, 2014, www.rogerebert.com/rogers-journal/a-viewers-companion-to-citizen-kane.

Franco, J. "Universalising Art: 'The Disaster Artist' And 'The Room,'" December 5, 2013, accessed on February 10, 2014, www.vice.com/en_uk/read/universalizing-art-the-disaster-artist-and-the-room.

Gettell, O. "James Franco Is James Franco, Yet Again," June 10, 2014, accessed on June 22, 2014, www.latimes.com/entertainment/movies/moviesnow/la-et-mn-james-franco-dave-room-lindsay-lohan-story-class-20140610-story.html.

"Greg Sestero AMA: The Sequel," February 23, 2014, accessed on February 25, 2014, www.reddit.com/r/IAmA/comments/1ynfhz/hi_reddit_its_greg_sestero_mark_from_the_room/.

Heisler, S. "Tommy Wiseau," June 24, 2009, accessed on March 10, 2014, www.avclub.com/article/tommy-wiseau-29598.

Knegt, P. "The Room" Director Tommy Wiseau Says a Sitcom and a Vampire Movie are Next: The Interview, Part 2," June 10 2011, accessed on March 10 2014, www.indiewire.com/article/tommy_wiseau_part_2.

Masnick, M. "Pissing Off a Movie Critic By Claiming Copyright Over A Video Review . . . Probably Not Smart," July 22, 2010, accessed on February 15, 2014, www.techdirt.com/articles/20100721/15284610310.shtml.

O'Neal, S. "Tommy Wiseau Planning *The Room* 3-D," December 21, 2010, accessed on March 11, 2014, www.avclub.com/article/tommy-wiseau-planning-ithe-room-3-d-i-49344.

Orlikoff, D. "Wiseau is in 'The Room," January 2014, accessed on May 2, 2014, www.columbiachronicle.com/arts_and_culture/article_b7c65dbd-8a19-5ebc-97a9-242572a96964.html?mode=jqm.

RCarstairs, IMDb review "This film is like getting stabbed in the head," June 28, 2003, accessed on March 2, 2014, www.imdb.com/user/ur2424961/.

Rose, S. "Is this the worst movie ever made?" *The Guardian,* September 10, 2009, accessed February 16 2014, www.theguardian.com/film/filmblog/2009/sep/10/cinema-the-room-cult.

United States Census Bureau, accessed on March 14 2014, www.census.gov/census2000/states/us.html.

Websites

The official *The Room* website, www.theroommovie.com/.

The official *The Room* store, www.theroommovie.com/buydirect.html.

The official *The Room* Facebook page, www.facebook.com/theroommovie.

The Room Fansite, www.theroomfansite.com/.

The Room Reddit sub-site, www.reddit.com/r/theroom/.

The Room Denmark official page, accessed on February 20, 2014, www.theroommovie.com/denmark.html.

The Neigbors official site, accessed on March 15, 2014, www.theneighborssitcom.com.

The Room: The Musical official site, accessed on March 3, 2014, http://whatisph.com/theroom/index.html.

Juliette Danielle's Facebook, uploaded on March 30, 2013, accessed on April 22, 2014, www.facebook.com/juliettedanielle.

The Prince Charles Cinema Events listings, accessed on February 4, 2014, www. princecharlescinema.com/events/events.php?seasonanchor=roomlive.

The *Room Full of Spoons* official website, accessed on May 10, 2014, www. roomfullofspoons.com/.

The official Razzies website, accessed on April 30, 2014, www.razzies.com.

James Franco official Instagram page, accessed on April 13, 2014 http://instagram.com/p/kl_1EBy9ab/.

The *Room Tribute* at Newgrounds, accessed on February 5, 2013, www. newgrounds.com/portal/view/547307.

JohnnyUtah, Newgrounds, accessed on May 1, 2014, http://johnnyutah. newgrounds.com/.

Videos/Podcasts

The official Wiseau-Films YouTube Channel, accessed on February 20 2014, www.youtube.com/user/TheWiseauFilms.

The Tommy Wi-Show YouTube Channel, accessed on March 3 2014, www. youtube.com/show/thetommywishow.

Tommy Explains it All YouTube Channel, accessed on March 14, 2014, www. youtube.com/user/TommyExplainsItAll.

"*The Room:* Director's Edition," episode 23 of *How Did This Get Made?* November 15, 2011, accessed on February 20, 2014, www.earwolf.com/episode/the-room-directors-edition/.

"The Room—The Flower Shop Scene," uploaded June 13 2009, accessed 15 February 2014, www.youtube.com/watch?v=7S9Ew3TIeVQ.

Red Letter Media—Star Wars Episode I: The Phantom Menace, accessed on March 14, 2014, http://redlettermedia.com/plinkett/star-wars/star-wars-episode-1-the-phantom-menace/.

"Tommy Wiseau's "The Neighbors" Trailer," uploaded Jan 13 2009, accessed Feb 15 2014, www.youtube.com/watch?v=YGpwxHMUndk.

"Tommy Wiseau Interview Part 2" uploaded April 14, 2011, accessed on February 13, 2014, www.youtube.com/watch?v=2EjDCkPALOs.

"Tommy Wiseau Gets Hit by Football" uploaded on January 9, 2011, accessed on February 23, 2014, www.youtube.com/watch?v=siQ8zTCEOc4.

"CNN Interview—'The Room,'" uploaded August 16, 2011, accessed April 13, 2014, www.youtube.com/watch?v=kEfJ4jEH69A.

"Bristol Bad Film Club's Question to Tommy Wiseau and Greg Sestero at the Prince Charles Cinema," uploaded on February 10, 2014, accessed on February 24, 2014, www.youtube.com/watch?v=3JyjPiSVF1w.

"Tommy Wiseau recites a sonnet," uploaded on March 21, 2009, accessed on March 14, 2014, www.youtube.com/watch?v=-76HUrNa15Q.

"Tommy Wiseau & Greg Sestero (THE ROOM) LIVE with Beth and Videogum" uploaded August 3, 2013, accessed on February 17, 2014, www.youtube. com/watch?v=e6RtfG7D5dY.

"'The Room'—THE ORIGINAL OPENING TITLES THEME" uploaded October 29, 2013, accessed on April 22, 2014, www.youtube.com/watch?v=iS4QJImQnfo.

Playboy Adventures—"Episode 2," uploaded May 28 2006, accessed on March 1 2014, www.channel101.com/episode/384.

"Tommy Wiseau Wishes YOU A Happy Memorial Day!" May 23 2013, accessed on February 10 2014, www.youtube.com/watch?v=R799vrY6zVA.

"THE DISASTER ARTIST: My Life Inside THE ROOM, the Greatest Bad Movie Ever Made," uploaded September 20 2013, accessed on March 15 2014, www.youtube.com/watch?v=Eh9IC7IBJvI.

"Oh Hi, Mark! An Evening with Greg Sestero: The Disaster Artist" uploaded on December 30 2013, accessed on March 13 2014, www.youtube.com/watch?v=e5Vl1DuKmL8#t=29.

"Seth Rogen talks Cult Movie, The Room" uploaded on May 8 2014, accessed on May 10 2014, www.youtube.com/watch?v=GYI60SxpYMY.

Rifftrax *The Room* audio commentary, June 18 2009, www.rifftrax.com/rifftrax/room.

"Nostalgia Critic—The Room," uploaded on December 20 2010, accessed on April 15 2014, www.youtube.com/watch?v=gsgIq7cxhJk.

"The Tommy Wiseau Interview!" September 27 2011, accessed on 10 April 2014, http://proudlyresents.com/tommyw/.

"The Room Neck Scene Redux," uploaded February 25 2011, accessed 27 April 2014, www.youtube.com/watch?v=7IYUPmx4EHo.

"Tommy Wiseau's The Room rap," uploaded March 17 2009, accessed February 2 2014, www.youtube.com/watch?v=Kx-FcOiVF2A.

"How to Play a Drug Dealer (with Tommy Wiseau)," uploaded on June 11 2011, accessed on May 1 2014, www.youtube.com/watch?v=jrxIht0SPXc.

"The Room—performed live—with Greg Sestero," uploaded on November 16 2013, accessed on April 3 2014, www.youtube.com/watch?v=rq3yvgUeGmk.

"Tommy Wiseau announces his next film, "Foreclosure,"" uploaded on June 15, 2012, accessed on April 20, 2014, www.youtube.com/watch?v=iC4O4ERRGTU.

Filmography

Aliens Dir. James Cameron, 20th Century Fox, 1986; 20th Century Fox, 2004, DVD.

Back to the Future Dir. Robert Zemeckis, Universal, 1985; Universal Pictures UK, 2013, Blu-ray.

Basket Case Dir. Frank Henenlotter, Analysis Film Releasing Corporation 1982; Second Sight Films, 2012, DVD.

Being There Dir. Hal Ashby, United Artists, 1979, Warner Home Video, 2009; Blu-ray.

Best Worst Movie Dir. Michael Stephenson, Magicstone Productions, 2009; New Video Group, 2010, DVD.

Birdemic: Shock and Terror James Nguyen, Severin Films, 2010; Severin, 2011, DVD.

Bullitt Dir. Peter Yates, Warner Bros. 1968; Warner Home Video, 2007, Blu-ray.

Citizen Kane Dir. Orson Welles, Mercury Productions/RKO Radio Pictures, 1941; Warner Bros. 2011, Blu-ray.

Crank Dirs.Neveldine/Taylor, Lionsgate, 2006; UCA, 2011, DVD.

Dark Knight, The Dir. Christopher Nolan, Warner Bros. Pictures, 2008; Warner Home Video, 2008, DVD.

Dirty Harry Dir. Don Siegel, Warner Bros. 1971; Warner Home Video, 2009, Blu-ray.

Exorcist, The Dir. William Friedkin, Warner Bros. 1973; Warner Home Video, 2013, Blu-ray.

First Blood Dir. Ted Kotcheff, Orion Pictures, 1982; Studiocanal, 2008, DVD.

First Wives Club, The Dir. Hugh Wilson, Paramount Pictures, 1996; Paramount Home Entertainment, 2000, DVD.

(500) Days of Summer Dir. Marc Webb, Fox Searchlight Pictures, 2009; 20th Century Fox Home Entertainment, 2010, DVD.

Gigli Dir. Martin Brest, Columbia Pictures, 2003; UCA, 2005, DVD.

Godfather, The Dir. Francis Ford Coppola, Paramount Pictures, 1972; Paramount Home Entertainment, 2011, Blu-ray.

Hakuchi Dir. Akira Kurosawa, Shochiku, 1951; Eureka, 2005, DVD.

Homeless in America Dirs. Tommy Wiseau/Kaya Redford, Wiseau-Films, 2004; Wiseau-Films, 2004, DVD.

Howard the Duck Dir. Willard Huyck, Universal Pictures, 1986; Metrodome Distribution Ltd, 2008, DVD.

In the Mood for Love Dir. Wong Kar-Wai, USA Films. 2000; The Criterion Collection, 2012, Blu-ray.

James Dean Dir. Mark Rydell, Turner Network Television, 2001; Warner Home Video, 2005, DVD.

Last Tango in Paris Dir. Bernardo Bertolucci, United Artists, 1972; 20th Century Fox Home Entertainment, 2011, Blu-ray.

Leaving Las Vegas Dir. Mike Figgis, United Artists 1995; MGM, 2011, Blu-ray.

Little Shop of Horrors Dir. Frank Oz, Warner Bros.1986; Warner Home Video, 2013, Blu ray.

Love Story Dir. Arthur Hiller, Paramount Pictures, 1970; Paramount Home Entertainment, 2013.

Machete Dirs. Robert Rodriguez/Ethan Maniquis, 20th Century Fox, 2010; Sony Pictures Home Entertainment, 2011, DVD.

Maltese Falcon, The Dir. JohnHuston, Warner Bros. 1941, Warner Home Video, 2006, DVD.

Manos: The Hands of Fate Dir. Harold P.Warren, Emerson Film Enterprises, 1966; Alpha Video, 2003, DVD.

Mulholland Drive Dir. David Lynch, Universal Pictures, 2001; Optimum Home Entertainment, 2010, Blu-ray.

9½ Weeks Dir. Adrian Lyne, MGM, 1986; 20th Century Fox Home Entertainment, Blu-ray.

Paranormal Activity Dir. Oren Peli, Paramount Pictures. 2009; Icon Home Entertainment, 2010, DVD.

Pink Flamingos Dir. John Waters, Dreamland 1972; New Line Home Entertainment, 2001, DVD.

Plan 9 from Outer Space Dir. Ed Wood, Valiant Pictures, 1959; Legend Films, 2012, Blu-ray.

Pulp Fiction Dir. Quentin Tarantino, Miramax Films, 1994; Lions Gate Home Entertainment, 2011, Blu-ray.

Reality Check Dir. Rafael Zielinski, Nu Image Films, 2002; Universal Home Video, 2004, DVD.

Rebel Without a Cause Dir. Nicholas Ray, Warner Bros.1955; Warner Home Video, 2006, DVD.

Reefer Madness Dir. Louis J. Gasnier, Motion Picture Ventures, 1936; Legend Films, 2008, DVD.

Ringu Dir. Hideo Nakata, Toho Company Ltd., 1998; Tartan, 2001, DVD.

Rocky Horror Picture Show, The Dir. Jim Sharman, 20th Century Fox, 1975; 20th Century Fox Home Entertainment, 2010, Blu-ray.

Room, The Dir. Tommy Wiseau, Wiseau-Films, 2003; Wiseau-Films, 2005, DVD/2012, Blu-ray.

Searchers, The Dir. John Ford, Warner Bros. 1956; Warner Home Video, 2006, Blu-ray.

Sharknado Dir. Anthony C. Ferrante, The Asylum, 2013; Optimum Home Entertainment, 2013, DVD.

Showgirls Dir. Paul Verhoeven, United Artists, 1995; 20th Century Fox, 2003, DVD.

Snakes on a Plane Dir. David R. Ellis, New Line Cinema, 2006; Entertainment in Video, 2009, Blu-Ray.

Spring Breakers Dir. Harmony Korine, A24, 2012; Universal Pictures UK, 2013, Blu-ray.

Stalker Dir. Andrei Tarkovsky, Mosfilm, 1979; Artificial Eye, 2002, DVD.

Stand by Me Dir. Rob Reiner, Columbia Pictures 1986; Sony Pictures Home Entertainment, 2011, Blu-ray.

Star Wars Dir. George Lucas, 20th Century Fox, 1977; 20th Century Fox Home Entertainment, 2011, Blu-ray.

Star Wars Episode I: The Phantom Menace Dir. George Lucas, 20th Century Fox, 1999; 20th Century Fox Home Entertainment, 2011, Blu-ray.

Star Wars Episode II: Attack of the Clones Dir. George Lucas, 2002; 20th Century Fox Home Entertainment, 2011, Blu-ray.

Streetcar Named Desire, A Dir. Elia Kazan, Warner Bros. 1951, Warner Home Video, 2013, Blu-ray.

Sunset Boulevard Dir. Billy Wilder, Paramount Pictures, 1950; Paramount Home Entertainment, 2013, Blu-ray.

Superman Dir. Richard Donner, Warner Bros, 1978; Warner Home Video, 2011, Blu-ray.

The Talented Mr. Ripley, The Dir. Anthony Minghella, Miramax Films 1999; Optimum Home Entertainment, 2011, Blu-ray.

Terminator, The Dir. James Cameron, Orion Pictures, 1984; 20th Century Fox Home Entertainment, 2012, Blu-ray.

There Will Be Blood Dir. Paul Thomas Anderson, Miramax Films, 2007; Warner Bros., 2008, Blu-ray.

Tokyo Story Dir. Yasujiro Ozu, Shochiku, 1953; BFI, 2010, Blu-ray.

Tomorrow Never Dies Dir. Roger Spottiswoode, United International Pictures, 1997; MGM, 2003, DVD.

Transformers: Revenge of the Fallen Dir. Michael Bay, Paramount Pictures, 2009; Paramount Home Entertainment, 2009, DVD.

Troll 2 Dir. Claudio Fragasso, Epic Productions, 1990; MGM, 2010, Blu-ray.

Usual Suspects, The Dir. Bryan Singer, Polygram Filmed Entertainment, 1995; 20th Century Fox, 2007, DVD.

Vertigo Dir. Alfred Hitchcock, Paramount Pictures, 1958; Universal Pictures UK, 2013, Blu-ray.

Wolf of Wall Street, The Dir. Martin Scorsese, Paramount Pictures, 2013; Universal Pictures, 2014, Blu-ray.

Television
AFI Life Achievement Award: A Tribute to George Lucas Dir. Louis J.Horvitz, TNT, 2005.
Breaking Bad AMC/Netflix, 2008–13.
Garth Marenghi's Darkplace Dir. Richard Ayoade, Channel Four, 2004.
Mystery Science Theater 3000 KTMA/Comedy Central/The Comedy Channel/ The Sci-Fi Channel, 1988–99.
South Park Comedy Central, 1997–present.
Tim and Eric Awesome Show, Great Job! Adult Swim, 2007–10.